JOSH McDOWELL

Bestselling author of *Evidence That Demands a Verdict*

J E S U S:
DEAD OR ALIVE?

TEEN EDITION
EVIDENCE FOR THE
RESURRECTION
with Ariel Allison

SEAN McDOWELL

Regal

From Gospel Light
Ventura, California, U.S

Published by Regal
From Gospel Light
Ventura, California, U.S.A.
www.regalbooks.com
Printed in the U.S.A.

Library of Congress Cataloging-in-Publication Data
McDowell, Josh.
Jesus : dead or alive? / Josh McDowell and Sean McDowell with Ariel Allison.
p. cm.
Includes bibliographical references.
ISBN 978-0-8307-4787-0 (trade paper)
1. Jesus Christ—Resurrection. I. McDowell, Sean. II. Allison, Ariel. III. Title.
BT482.M34 2009
232'.5—dc22
2008046382

1 2 3 4 5 6 7 8 9 10 11 12 13 14 15 / 15 14 13 12 11 10 09

Rights for publishing this book outside the U.S.A. or in non-English languages
are administered by Josh McDowell Ministry, a division of Campus Crusade
for Christ International. For additional information, please visit www.josh.org,
email translations@josh.org, or write to Josh McDowell Ministry, 660 International
Parkway Suite 100, Richardson, TX 75081.

CONTENTS

1

SO WHAT?

Mary hurried through the silvery darkness as the first glimmers of dawn began to stretch across the sky. Her face was down, the hood of her robe shielding her flushed cheeks and pained expression. Under one arm was tucked a bundle of neatly folded cloth strips and under the other, a clay pot filled with thick, waxy perfume. She knew this task would turn her stomach and trouble her nostrils. His body had been in the cave for three days.

Mary left the narrow alleys of the city and made her way into quieter residential areas where wealthy families still slumbered. She soon spilled out the open gate and made her way along the road that led from Jerusalem. Her sandals slapped against her bare feet as she rushed along the hard packed soil. *Thwap, thwap, thwap.* After walking a short distance, Mary veered off into an olive vineyard, the broad flat leaves pungent in the crisp air.

As she approached her destination, her pace slowed and her will faltered. There was no joy in the task that lay before her, only a crippling sorrow that threatened to suck the marrow from her bones.

"Give me courage, Lord," she whispered through parted lips.

Nearing her destination, Mary stopped on the path and took a deep breath, a shudder running through her body.

Anywhere but here. Not now. Surely I can't do this. I can't see his face again . . . the pain . . . the sorrow.

Yet the thought of leaving his body in the cave, bloodied and bruised, was more unbearable than the burial dressing she was about to perform. Mary took a step forward, and then another.

She continued slowly, until she rounded the curve and beheld the grave where they laid the crucified body of her Lord. Until then it had not occurred to her how she would move the massive round stone that blocked the entrance to the tomb. But it didn't matter. Someone had already rolled the stone away. It sat to the side of the dark entrance. Like a missing tooth in a perfect smile, the black hole gaped at Mary as she stood dumbfounded on the path.

"Please let him be in there," she gasped, picking up the hem of her robes and running to the cave. It was empty, robbed of even the smell of death.

A small cry escaped her lips and she turned helplessly in the cave, searching for a body that wasn't there.

They have taken him.

Mary set the cloth strips and clay pot down gently, careful not to spill its contents, and then she bolted from the cave. There was no gentle flapping of her sandals as she ran back to the city, just the urgent pounding of her feet as desperation drove her forward. Her robe trailed behind her, and the waist-length braid she'd tucked inside her garments thumped against her back as she went in search of the only two men who could help: Peter and John, beloved friends of Jesus.

As Mary ran, lungs burning and tears pressing at the corners of her eyes, memories flooded her mind. A life spent used and abused by men seeking their own gratification. Years as an outcast, forced away from the company of women. Meeting the man called Jesus, and the day he cast seven demons from her. Devotion to this God-man, now dead, and the agony that washed over her as she sat beneath the cross, with his mother, weeping as his life drained away. Watching his limp body lowered to the ground and the kindness of a stranger who offered a new tomb.

These things seeped through Mary's mind as she rushed through the city gates and into the narrow streets. She wound her way upward by memory, her breath coming in wheezing gasps, until she reached the small home with a low wooden mantel. Mary charged through the door without knocking, and came to a stop in the middle of a low-ceilinged room crowded with sleeping men.

Two words made it through her lips as she gasped for air and held a hand against her chest, "He's gone!"

Merriam Webster's Dictionary defines the word "hinge" as a "determining factor" or "turning point." The death of Jesus Christ was the point upon which human history turned. For thousands of years, even our calendars were regulated by his life: B.C., Before Christ, and A.D., *anno domini,* or "the year of our Lord." Never before, or since, has the death of a single human being affected the world so dramatically.

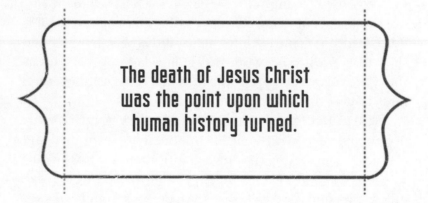

> The death of Jesus Christ was the point upon which human history turned.

But why? More than two thousand years later, why are we still talking about one dead Jewish man? After all, we live in troubling times. Two million people die of AIDS every year, over half of whom live in Africa. Babies are orphaned as their parents succumb to the disease. Women are widowed and forced to watch their children starve because they cannot feed them. Millions more suffer with the virus and wait their turn to die.

In the Middle East, war rages and threatens to unleash global violence. Countries debate the use of oil while the blood of terrorists and innocents alike is shed on sandy soil. Thousands of soldiers leave their families and many never return. Widows and orphans. Again. And, of course, our planet itself groans beneath the weight of human choices. We pollute. We destroy. We use and do not replenish.

The truth is that we don't have to list any of the above issues to demonstrate the hopelessness of our planet all these years after the death of Christ. We could look at the world through the eyes of the many unbelievers who also see the hurt, destruction and tragedies of life on earth as a meaningless existence. For example, consider the following comment posted on an Internet atheist website:

> I'm confused . . . I always believed science would be the cure-all for my problems, but I don't know if I can keep living without eternal life. I guess I'll just have to find a way myself to make it through this meaningless existence. I just wish I knew of someone who could show me the path to eternal life. If science can't provide the answers, though, then who or what can!? *sigh* Doesn't it seem like there is a higher power that gives our lives purpose? Well, science says there isn't, so there isn't.[1]

With our world like this, the turmoil and human anguish, why is the death of Jesus Christ even an issue? Why should we care that a 33-year-old man was tortured and murdered in ancient Palestine when such violence is a daily occurrence in our country, our states, and our home towns?

Everyone dies, whether a peasant in Africa or a millionaire on Wall Street. There is no way around our common fate. And the certainty of death is perhaps the greatest fear of mankind. It is fair to ask why *his* death was so special.

Far more than the fate of his disciples or even the fate of ancient Israel hung on the cross that day. The fate of the entire human race and their hope of life after death hung there with Christ. He was humanity's last hope. But with his death, hope was destroyed. Eternal life became a mere dream. Death would reign forever. The supposed Savior was dead, and any hope of deliverance would be buried with him. Yet it was not just his death that caused all of history to pivot in a new direction. It was what happened next . . .

Mary stood in the small room, still trying to catch her breath.

"What do you mean he's gone?" Peter asked, rising from the floor. His hair was disheveled and he looked as though he had slept where he had fallen the night before.

"I went to dress his body," she said, choking on her own words. "But the stone was moved and the tomb empty."

At this news a murmur ran through the room, and a second disciple, John, also rose to put on his sandals. These men were two of Jesus' closest friends and after his death, grief hit them the hardest.

"What are we going to do, Peter? They have taken his body!" Lines of worry streaked across her forehead and her mouth drew tight in concern.

"Take us to the tomb," he said, looking older and more sorrowful than she'd ever seen him. For the first time she noticed gray hairs embedded deep in his long beard and his dark brown eyes were sunken, tired.

The three heartbroken disciples left the house and meandered through the city. They neither spoke nor looked one another in the eyes, their thoughts on the empty tomb. With this turn of events all they hoped for as Christ-followers was destroyed. They and the small band of believers had believed Jesus would change the world for good.

But they soon found themselves in a state of mental and emotional anguish as they stood watching Jesus breathe his last on a Roman cross. He was the miracle worker who could command nature, heal sickness, raise the dead, and produce food with a word or gesture. They had given up everything to follow him. But now they were headed to a tomb that held his lifeless body. He was dead. And with him died all the hopes they placed in him.

Mary led them to the cave, darkness looming from within. Peter stood at the entrance, head down, resting a hand on the massive round stone. He and John slowly made their way into the tomb and looked around. The collapsed shell of the grave clothes was still intact, lying on the rock ledge, but the body was nowhere to be found. Peter shook his head and blinked back tears. Frightened and confused, he and John turned toward home without a word.

But Mary lingered behind. The emptiness in her heart was matched only by that of the tomb. Silent. Lonely. Comfortless. She gathered the strips of cloth and perfume she had left earlier. Mary turned her back to the darkness as tears began to slide down her cheeks. She stepped into the morning sunlight and allowed herself to weep without abandon. Before walking away, she peered back in the tomb for one last look, and what she saw startled her: two men, robed in bright white, sat inside the tomb.

She blinked, fearing the bright sunlight caused spots to float before her eyes. But the men remained.

"Why are you crying?" the angels asked.

She stood silent for a moment, unsure what to say. Seconds earlier she was in the tomb by herself and now she found herself trying to answer these strangers. "Because they have taken away my Lord," she replied, swallowing a gulp. "And I don't know where they have put him."

They looked past her and Mary turned to find another man outside the tomb, waiting patiently. She blinked a fresh set of tears from her eyes.

"Dear woman, why are you crying?" he asked, voice gentle and eyes kind.

"Sir, if you have taken him away, tell me where you have put him, and I will go and get him," she pleaded, taking a step toward the man she assumed was a gardener. Mary wanted to pay her final respects and lay her Lord to rest. The thought that his body was in the hands of his enemies made her heart ache all the more.

"Mary!" The man called her by name and held out a hand.

It took her only a moment to recognize his familiar voice. "Teacher!" she cried, as she recognized the man who stood outside the cave as Jesus himself. She rushed to him, throwing her arms around his neck, and weeping ecstatically.

Jesus stood before Mary alive, healthy and well. Not even death could hold the promised Savior.

When Christ died on the cross, it seemed all had been lost. Death won. But after three days in a rich man's tomb, Jesus appeared alive again. The news was so absurd his disciples refused to believe it until he presented himself to them and let them touch his wounds with their own hands. Then Jesus made an amazing claim to his disciples: In the future they too would have resurrected bodies like his. Bodies that would never deteriorate, age or perish. They would realize the one great hope that brought purpose to an otherwise meaningless existence. They would have new life without death or pain in the presence of a loving God forever.

This is the hope Jesus offers to a hopeless world—an afterlife with God, free of pain and suffering, filled with total joy. This is exactly how the Bible describes heaven, a place of unimaginable happiness.

"But," you may ask, "what does Christ's resurrection mean to *me*? Yes, I would like to have eternal life, but how does what *supposedly* happened to Christ give it to me? So he claims to have been raised from the dead. That's cool, if true, but ultimately, so what? What does the death and resurrection of a man two thousand years ago have to do with me in the twenty-first century?"

The promise of resurrection is this: What happened to Christ can happen for us. Like him, we will die, but his resurrection is a promise that death is not the end. His resurrection is the blueprint for our own. He blazed the trail through death to eternal life, and he tells us we can follow in his footsteps with his hand leading us the entire way. The resurrection gives us hope for a glorious, pain-free, death-free future. Our most outlandish dreams of peace, love and harmony *can* be fulfilled.

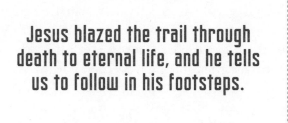

Jesus blazed the trail through death to eternal life, and he tells us to follow in his footsteps.

And the truth is, we long for what eternity promises. Life will never be perfect on this earth, even if all the problems we talked about earlier magically disappear. An AIDS vaccine will reduce suffering but it will not change the world. Wars and rumors of wars will always plague this planet, but they will never cease. The president of the United States can shape the direction of our country, but he cannot save mankind. God does call us to be good stewards of our planet, but he does not want us to worship it.

Yet the big questions remain: How can I be sure if all this is true? How can I know with confidence the resurrection really occurred? Maybe it's just another wishful dream. Christians claim it's true, but then, all religions claim their beliefs to be true. How can I know the resurrection will really happen?

2

IT'S THE END OF THE WORLD AS WE KNOW IT

The serpent crept up on Eve as she stood beneath the tree, resting in the shade of a perfect morning. Its branches arched in a canopy of greens and yellows, heavy laden with ripe fruit. Somewhere in the distance a swallow whistled greetings to a newly risen sun, and a hummingbird flitted from one red flower to the next, drinking nectar and filling the air with a gentle hum. Adam stood a few feet away from his wife, back turned as he watched a herd of bison graze in the tall grass. The serpent slithered toward the woman, careful to stay out of Adam's sight. He wanted to speak with the woman without interference.

The serpent slowly wound his bright green body around the tree trunk next to Eve until his pointed head became level with her clear blue eyes. "What have I heard?" he whispered in her ear. "Did God *really* say that you may not eat from any tree in this garden?" He watched her, carefully gauging whether she would detect the subtle twisting of God's command.

Eve turned and faced him with curiosity, her eyes large and trusting. Her hair fell in soft waves across her shoulders and down her back. Gentle fingers played with a stalk of grain and a ready smile turned the corners of her mouth heavenward. Of everything that lived in this garden, Eve represented the perfection of God's new creation most clearly and the serpent hated her for that.

She shook her head. "We can eat the fruit of any tree in the garden except *this one*," she said, lifting her eyes toward the branches a few feet above her head. "God said that we could not eat it, or even *touch* it, or we will die."

She exaggerates, he thought. *God never told them that they could not touch the tree. This is good.*

His tongue flickered in the corner of his mouth as a malicious grin crept across his face. His words oozed with sweetness, with lies. "Oh, surely you won't *die*." He leaned in closer, planting the words in her mind like ripe seeds in fertile soil. "God knows that when you eat this fruit your eyes will open and you will be *like Him*, knowing good and evil."

Adam turned to look at them and his eyes narrowed as he strained to hear the conversation. He left the animals and joined them in the shade.

Eve looked at her husband and then cast a glance toward the fruit that hung within arms reach. Her eyes opened wide as she looked at the soft red skin ready to burst with flavor and juice. The inviting aroma of tender fruit drifted down from the branches above, filling her nostrils with a promised sweetness.

Yes. Yesss. The serpent thought. *Take and eat. Eat and die.*

"It does look good," she muttered. "And you say it will make us wise?"

He nodded. "*Yesss.*"

She reached into the branches and pulled the nearest fruit. It dropped easily into her hands, heavy with juice. As she raised it to her mouth she gave her husband a final glance, but he stood beside her silently. Eve bit deeply into the tender skin, her mouth flooding with the taste of forbidden fruit.

The serpent watched with elation as she handed it to her husband. He could not help the triumphant laughter that spilled from his throat as Adam took and ate as well. And then he slowly unwound from the tree as he relished the look of horror that spread across their faces. The agony and the realization that this indulgence was poison to the body and soul filled their eyes first and then crept across their faces like a stain. The bitterness of their choice, the choice *he* so easily coaxed them into, became clear in an instant. Until that moment they knew only what God intended for them—good. But with a single bite they brought upon themselves the very thing the serpent desired that they experience—evil. The perfect world God created for mankind evaporated before their eyes.

Eve dropped the fruit, spitting what remained in her mouth to the grass. "But you said we would become wise . . ." she choked, turning to him with horror.

And then Adam spoke for the first time, too late. His voice a mere whisper, but one that would shout through all of history, "You lied."

Yessss, I lied, thought the serpent as he watched them, intoxicated with his own victory. *And I will lie to your sons and your daughters and every son of Adam and daughter of Eve that will ever walk this earth. The seed is planted and you will never rid your souls of the specter of death. God spoke truly to you in his command. You will surely die.*

You just met the single most despicable villain in history. The likes of Adolf Hitler, the Zodiac killer, Al Capone, Jeffrey Dahmer, Charles Manson and Jack the Ripper have nothing on that serpent—Satan. Though they littered human history with destruction and death, they modeled themselves after the one who originally brought horror to this earth. All lies, hatred and evil find their source in him.

We see the brutality of a ruined human nature not just on the pages of history but on the big screen as well. Some of the more famous movie villains also make us cringe: the Joker, Darth Vader, Freddy Krueger, Hannibal Lecter, and the Terminator all illustrate what human beings can do. The single goal of a villain is to kill, steal and destroy. They want to create misery and incite hatred. In that respect they follow their original leader. Such thoughts had not entered into the heart of man before that fateful day in the Garden of Eden, but they have haunted us ever since.

The truth of our world is that terrible things happen to innocent people. We try to build a good life, but our plans crumble, sometimes by death but often by unexpected events that catapult us into devastating circumstances. We will never experience the horrors of the Holocaust or the genocide in Sudan, but we all face unexpected fears, pain, disappointment and tragedy. We all deal with some form of suffering that sears itself into our memory: childhood sexual abuse, our parent's marriage ending in divorce, death of a loved one, a broken body, an unplanned pregnancy, drug addiction. These are the side affects of what happened when Eve ate the forbidden fruit and gave it to her husband. In that moment man pushed God away and the void remains crippling.

> **We will never experience the horrors of the Holocaust or the genocide in Sudan, but we all face unexpected fears, pain, disappointment and tragedy.**

Even this dusty earth feels the pain of trouble and death. It groans under the stress of a cursed world. Disasters occur every day. One glimpse at the evening news leaves us wondering how our world manages to keep spinning. Tornadoes wreak havoc on life and property, babbling brooks flood their banks to become

destructive forces, and the friendly flicker of a campfire trans-
forms into a raging forest inferno, consuming plants, animals
and homes. Earthquakes. Tornadoes. Hurricanes. Tsunamis.
Our world assaults us at every turn. Animals that once roamed the
earth in harmony now brutally ravage each other to survive and
protect their territory. Mountains erupt, spewing volcanic ash.
The sun parches fields, bringing drought, ruin and more death.

These harsh realities coexist in stark contrast with glimpses
of joy and beauty. We have people in our lives that we love and
who love us in return. This world, so broken with tragedy, also
gives us glimpses of glory. We see so much good in this world,
why must it be marred by all the pain, tragedy and death that
dog us so relentlessly?

Because of all that we endure it seems that such evil has always
been part of our existence, but that is actually not the case.

The pain, tragedy and death that wreak havoc on us were unknown in God's original creation. The beauty we see in nature,
the joy we experience in loving relationships, and the pleasure we
experience in so many ways hint at what the world looked like
when God first placed Adam and Eve in that garden. Pride, lust,
greed and jealousy had no place in our relationships. Destructive
storms, droughts and forest fires never troubled the earth with
their ferocity. Parents didn't get divorced, and family members
didn't die. Death, pain and sickness had no place in God's original creation. Everything worked just as it should, instead of
falling apart at the seams with pollution and abuse.

That may sound like a drug-induced apparition—a fantasy of
our own imagining that oozes with improbability. But each of us
wonders if this world, complex though it is, was put together by
a higher power. And a being powerful enough to invent pleasure,
love, happiness and joy surely would have the ability to prevent

the evils that infect us now. How could everything be perfect and pain-free, as in the world described above, and then degenerate into the pain and death-ravaged world we experience now?

Things went well for the human race for a time. Pain, tragedy, ruin and death could never invade the world as long as Adam and Eve chose to remain in their loving relationship with God. As long as they *chose* . . .

Adam and Eve may never have stepped away from God if Satan kept his distance. It was a simple thing he did really, getting them to doubt God's goodness. "Did God *really* say . . .?" A single question caused them to follow their own desires instead of God's plan.

No doubt, they did not consider the devastating consequences of their choice in advance. And as a result of that one decision, everything changed. Yet God honored their choice. He got out of their lives and didn't interfere with the independence and freedom they chose, and in His absence evil began to reign. Where God is absent, evil takes over, whether in the hearts of men or the world at large.

This event—the choice of the first human couple to reject God and trust themselves—is called sin. This "religious" sounding word simply means to do something that we shouldn't. Sin comes in many varieties, from the tiny, seemingly insignificant act of going over the speed limit to the appalling sin of mass murder. Yet one thing remains common to all sins, from the least to the greatest. They spring from the original impulse of Adam and Eve to follow their own desires instead of God's. All sin rejects the way of God in favor of self. It has the effect of a nuclear bomb exploding in our hearts. Depending on the sin, the blast field varies, but it always brings chaos, pain, tragedy and death.

CONSIDER THIS

If Satan intended to bring chaos to God's creation, one would think he succeeded. He wanted the first man and woman to pull away from God, and then all their descendants would inherit their desperation. Since God is the source of all life, separation from him means death. Adam and Eve doomed humanity by their choice to reject God. As Paul tells us, "When Adam sinned, sin entered the world. Adam's sin brought death, so death spread to everyone, for everyone sinned" (Romans 5:12). At the Fall of Adam and Eve, death entered God's perfect world and ruined all humankind.

If Satan intended to bring chaos to God's creation, one would think he succeeded. He wanted the first man and woman to pull away from God, and then all their descendants would inherit their desperation.

Since God is the source of all life, separation from him means death. Adam and Eve doomed humanity by their choice to reject God. As Paul tells us, "When Adam sinned, sin entered the world. Adam's sin brought death, so death spread to everyone, for everyone sinned" (Romans 5:12). At the Fall of Adam and Eve, death entered God's perfect world and ruined all humankind.

The burning flush of shame crept over Eve's cheeks as she stood holding the fruit in her limp hand. Tears pressed into the corners of her eyes as she looked at the serpent, so smug and triumphant. Just moments ago the light in the garden drifted between the branches, golden and pure. Now it seemed stifled, muted with the destruction of her choice.

For the first time Eve realized that she stood in the midst of the garden, naked. A deeper shade of red flushed her face and she pulled into the shadows, seeking to hide. Adam darted into the bushes beside her and they sat in the dirt, grabbing fig leaves from a nearby tree and weaving them into a covering. She kept her eyes away from Adam's face, fearful of what she would find there. They both knew that she had eaten first and they both knew that he did not stop her. Her heart struggled with a deep shame at her part and a growing anger at his. Both emotions were foreign and terrifying.

And then they heard the voice they feared most. Not that of the crafty serpent who had seduced them with lies, but the voice of God, the same voice that told them not to eat of the tree.

"Quick," Adam said, grabbing her arm and pulling her deeper into the bushes. "Hide."

She followed him farther into the brambles and they sat beneath the leaves like guilty children hiding from a parent.

"Where are you?" he called to them.

Eve knew it was rhetorical. He knew where they hid and he knew why. He waited for them in the sunshine, waited for them to crawl into the light and confess. Both she and Adam knew in that moment that cowering would do no good. They could not hide from God. Slowly they emerged from the shadows, faces burning and heads hung low. They avoided his gaze and instead they stood before him, shifting their feet and wringing their hands.

Finally, Adam spoke. "I heard you and I was afraid because I'm naked. So I hid."

Kindness resonated in God's voice even though they could not bear to search for it in his eyes. "Who told you that? Have you eaten from the tree?"

And then Adam turned to her, a look on his face she'd never seen before. His brow furrowed and he pointed an accusing finger. His voice burned with venom. "This woman that *you* gave me as a wife ate the fruit and gave it to me."

Anger, sudden and fierce, welled in her heart. Had Adam not been standing there while the serpent whispered to her? Had she not looked to him for direction? And now he stood there before God, placing the blame entirely on her shoulders after he left her defenseless.

"What have you done?" God asked, his words boring a hole into her heart.

And she knew, more than any moment before, what consequences her choice brought upon them. But even now she shut her heart to that truth and folded her arms across her chest. She would not look him in the eyes. "That serpent deceived me and I ate," she muttered, desperate to place blame anywhere but where it belonged, just as Adam had done. Then she raised a hand, still dripping with juice, and pointed at the serpent, only a few feet away.

The air crackled with tension as he turned to the serpent. It cowered, no longer laughing. His voice thundered through the garden, resounding like thunder. "Because you have done this, you are *cursed* more than any beast. You will live on your belly and dust will be your food for all the days of your life. I am declaring war between you and the Woman, between your off- spring and hers. He will wound your head, and you will wound his heel."

His words were a riddle to her mind, unfathomable. But she knew they were profound because the serpent shrunk away, writhing not just on his belly but twisting with anger. Something transpired between them as the curse was spoken, something that hinted to the fact that things may not have gone the serpent's way entirely.

As God turned from the serpent, Eve wanted to run, wanted to escape. For she knew that she would be next.

He cast his eyes upon her and she felt the weight of them in her soul. "I will greatly increase your pain in childbirth. In *pain* you will bring your children into this world. You will seek to con- trol your husband but he will rule over you."

She did not have the strength to argue or cry; she simply let the words fall upon her like shrapnel, piercing her heart.

"Because you have listened to the voice of your wife," he said to Adam, "and have eaten from the tree after I told *you* not to, I curse the earth because of you. You will labor all the days of your life and toil to grow food among the weeds. By the sweat of your face you will work, and then you will return to the earth as dust. I made you from dust and you shall return to dust."

And so they were cursed. In their marriage. With their chil- dren. Every form of human relationship doomed to suffer from their choice. And not only them, but all who would come after them and also the very ground on which they walked would suf- fer. It was the single worst moment of Eve's life, and the moment to which all of humanity would spit her name with shaking fist.

Cursed not only with a new nature, one of sin, but with physical
death as well . . .

The story of Adam and Eve often leaves us wondering why God
would punish *us* for something *they* did. It seems a bit unfair at
times. Why do I have to live in this brutal world just because they
ate that stupid fruit? If that was the extent of it, we might have
reason to argue our case. But the truth remains that each of us
has stood in their place countless times in our lives and chosen
something forbidden instead of God. We have each made up our
mind to doubt God's goodness.

"Did he *really* say not to have sex until I'm married? He just
doesn't want me to have any fun!"

"Did he *really* say that I shouldn't take that cash from
my dad's wallet? Well, he must not know how stingy my dad
can be!"

"Did he *really* say that I shouldn't cheat on that Algebra test?
Everyone else does it. God doesn't understand."

"Did he *really* say . . . ?"

Yes, he did, and just like Adam and Eve, we *choose* not to believe him. We have no grounds to argue that we are punished for
someone else's sin. We are punished for our own.

But if God loves us, as he says he does, why would he let
something like sin stand between us? He's God, after all, and he's
all-powerful, isn't he? Why can't he just forget that we sin and
save us anyway?

What if a judge failed to administer justice in his court?
What if you got a new car for your sixteenth birthday and someone keyed it? Now, imagine a judge, when hearing the case,
decided to let the guilty party go free because he wanted to act
lovingly! What would you think about him ignoring this crime?
How would your family feel? Naturally, you would cry out for

justice. Letting the vandal off would trivialize the crime and ignore the fact that justice must be done. What kind of world would we live in if every judge chose to "act lovingly and kindly" and forgive crimes instead of administering justice? It would be a great deal worse than the world where we live today.

God is the judge of the universe—the ultimate moral authority (see Genesis 18:25). His laws are fair; they stem from his very character and nature. Sin ignites God's wrath because it brings deep pain to those he loves. And because he has no sin, he cannot tolerate hatred, violence or injustice. If he did, he could not be good. He would not be God. Just as our eyes burn when we look at the sun, there is something within God's nature that causes him to burn with anger at the sight of evil.

> **Because God has no sin, he cannot tolerate hatred, violence or injustice. If he did, he could not be good. He would not be God.**

The sin of Adam and Eve and their subsequent fall left each of us with a serious dilemma. We have turned our backs on God and in so doing we have invited death into our lives. The first man and woman chose to believe Satan's lie that they could be like God—that their disobedience would make life better. Adam and Eve found that having sinned once, it gripped them like an addiction. Like a Meth addict, they couldn't stop using, and they passed on that terrible craving to all of their descendants. So now we all sin, and left to ourselves we are unable to break the habit.

The crisis in our culture illustrates this truth. Have you ever been so hurt, depressed or lonely that you seriously contemplated suicide? If so, you are not alone. According to a recent study, 20 percent of high school kids contemplated suicide over the past year, while 8 percent said they attempted suicide in the same time period. Twelve percent of kids are lonely, 25 percent feel unfulfilled in life, and nearly 50 percent say they are stressed out.[1] Many struggle with depression, feelings of loneliness, and rejection. There is nothing in our society that indicates our addiction to sin has made life better.

Youth ministry expert Dr. Chap Clark says in his book *Hurt: Inside the World of Today's Teenagers*, "Every single young person who has grown up in America is only one major event or catastrophe away from falling over the edge into what most would call at-risk."[2]

From an early age, we believe that we must possess extraordinary good looks, money, and moral compromise to achieve happiness. It is hardly surprising that so many of us take antidepressants, ADD meds, or steal prescription drugs from our parent's medicine cabinet. We hide our sadness in eating disorders, alcohol or random sexual hookups. In a rush to provide ourselves with everything, we've forgotten to answer a basic question: *Why are we here?*

Our cultural mantra can be summed up as, "Be yourself, believe in yourself, express yourself." Self, self, self! It's all about the self. Do you see the connection between our self-emphasis and the sin of Adam and Eve? It is essentially the same sin—the rejection of God's love and direction in favor of following our own desires and setting our own path.

In his book *Soul Searching*, Christian Smith observes that most youth view God as a cosmic therapist who exists to meet *their* needs rather than understanding their purpose as loving God and other people. Smith concludes, "As far as we could discern, what most teens appear to believe is that religion is about God responding to the authoritative desires and feelings of people . . . religion is essentially a tool for people to use to get what they want."[3] Is this true for you? If you are really honest with yourself, do you view God this way?

So the big question is, how do we find our way back to God? We have alienated ourselves from him, and he honored that choice by leaving us on our own, cut off from direction and hope. And we are doomed to remain in that condition unless God himself opens a way to come back to him. Since we are under judgment from his perfect justice, and since he is too good to tolerate our sin, how can we who are *addicted* to sin possibly get back in his good graces? We are doomed unless he provides a way.

3

LOVE IS A VERB

Fog settled into the garden, hovering over the damp earth like fallen moonlight. A gentle breeze swept along the ground, swirling the mist around a shrouded figure as he knelt beneath an olive tree, rocking back and forth. His lips moved silently as he gripped his hands together in prayer. A short distance away lay three men, slumbering comrades, too tired to watch with him through the darkness of this night.

"Let this cup pass from me," he whispered, beads of bloodied sweat dripping from his furrowed brow. "Nevertheless, let your will be done."

Even though his human flesh wanted to escape the brutal fate that awaited him in the coming hours, he remembered a promise given many years ago in another garden.

I'm declaring war between you and the Woman, between your offspring and hers. He'll wound your head, you'll wound his heel.

He rocked back on his heals and turned his face heavenward. A spattering of stars poked holes in the fabric of night like pin pricks in a bed sheet. In the distance the pounding of feet and the chink of armor invaded the garden. He turned and peered through the trees, catching a glimmer of torchlight. A small retinue of guards and servants of the High Priest marched through the grove of olive trees towards him.

"So it begins," he whispered, filling his lungs with air and his heart with resolve. He went to his friends and quickly roused them from sleep. "What are you doing? Get up and pray." The three men scrambled to their feet as they saw the approaching torchlight.

Steal spiked boots fell like hammers on the hard packed clay as a group of guards jogged along the path towards him. Within moments the soldiers surrounded them, pressing them together so they could not escape. Off to the side stood a servant come to ensure that his master's bidding was done.

He stepped into the path and asked, "Who are you looking for?"

"A man named Jesus, from Nazareth."

"I am Jesus," he said, raising his hands in surrender.

The guards looked at him as he stood before them, unassuming, dressed in a simple robe and sandals. Unsure of what to do, they shifted back and forth and whispered amongst themselves.

"He doesn't look like a criminal."

"*This* is the man we came to get?"

"Who are you looking for?" Jesus asked again, his voice echoing through the garden with strength and determination.

"We came for Jesus of Nazareth," the head guard repeated, his voice wavering with uncertainty.

"I told you," he said, "that's me. So if I'm the one you're after, let these others go." He nodded toward his friends, indicating they had no part in this.

At the back of the group stood a man he recognized, a man who had shared a meal with him just hours earlier. As their eyes met, Judas stepped forward. "Teacher!" he said, and then brushed his mouth against Jesus' cheek, the hotness of his breath a branding iron of betrayal. As he pulled away, the soldiers rushed forward to seize Jesus with drawn swords.

Then a blur of motion brushed by him as Peter drew a sword and lunged at the nearest person. The blade rose and fell before anyone could respond. And then the shriek of a wounded man pierced the still evening air.

"Put your sword away," Jesus ordered Peter. "Those who live by the sword will die by the sword. Don't you think that if I only asked, God would send a legion of angels to save me right now?"

Then he turned to the guards. "Why do you come after me with swords and clubs as if I were a dangerous criminal? Day after day I have been sitting in the Temple teaching, and you never so much as lifted a hand against me. You've done it this way to confirm everything Scripture says."

No sooner had the words slipped from his mouth than his three friends realized what was happening and bolted from the garden. Jesus found himself facing his accusers alone.

He crept forward and met the young servant where he crouched on the ground, a hand pressed against the bloodied wound where his right ear had been. He looked at Jesus, fear etched across his face, and shrunk away.

"Take heart, Malchus," he whispered, placing a hand gently against the wound.

Malchus looked at him, eyes spread wide as the flow of blood ceased. Jesus smiled slightly as the guards jerked him to his feet and bound his hands with shackles. He held the gaze of the stunned man, his eyes flooded with the mercy he freely offered. Even as they dragged him from the garden, the young man stayed behind, his expression a mixture of fear and awe.

One of the first evidences of God's redemptive love was given to Adam and Eve as they stood facing judgment for their sin. Even before telling them of all the pain and agony they would endure as a result of turning from him, he announced his plan to save them from their headlong plunge into death. In Genesis 3:15 God cursed the serpent, saying, "And I will cause hostility between you and the woman, and between your offspring and her offspring. He will strike your head, and you will strike his heel." This mysterious prophecy told them that a descendant of Eve would eventually come into the world and crush Satan's head, destroying forever the grip of death he inflicted upon the human race. In the process, this descendant would be wounded, his heel stricken, but the man would crush the serpent's head.

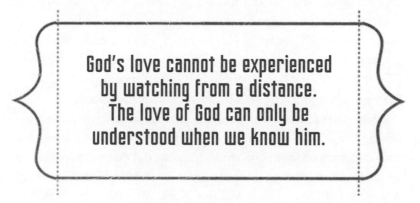

God's love cannot be experienced by watching from a distance. The love of God can only be understood when we know him.

Even more amazing, however, is the fact that he had devised the plan long before setting Adam and Eve in the garden. In 1 Peter 1:19-20 we read, "It was the precious blood of Christ, the sinless, spotless lamb of God. God chose him as your ransom long before the world began, but he has now revealed him to you in these last days." Here we see the true depth of God's love for us. Even before we sinned, he loved us so much that he had already devised a way to save us if we fell. And that plan involved a huge sacrifice on God's part. He intended to take the penalty for our sin upon himself, face death nose to nose, and defeat its power over us once and for all. Although greatly wounded in the process, he would ultimately conquer Satan.

Understanding the meaning of love begins by looking at the character of God rather than consulting a dictionary. "This is real love—not that we loved God, but that he loved us and sent his Son as a sacrifice to take away our sins" (1 John 4:10).

God's love cannot be experienced by watching from a distance. Love is realized in relationship, which means the love of God can only be understood when we know him. We can't just sit on the bleachers while God is on the field. If we truly want to experience his love, we must get in the game.

The great writer Ralph Waldo Emerson understood how important it is to give ourselves. He said, "A gift is an excuse for *not* giving yourself." Think about a father that only gives his children stuff instead of his time. It's little more than bribery. But a father who really loves his child will spend time with him, talking and building a relationship. He will give *himself*. This giving of self is exactly what God did for us in sending Jesus Christ. God gave *himself* as the substitute for our punishment.

Since the essence of love is self-giving, when God gave himself to mankind, he demonstrated the greatest and most astounding act of love in history. Jesus said, "For God loved the world so much that he gave his one and only Son, so that everyone who believes in him will not perish but have eternal life" (John 3:16). Every act of love in history pales in comparison to the gift of Jesus. No one took his life. He gave it willingly.

Flickering light from the small fire licked the stone walls like a hungry animal cleaning scraps from beneath a table. Though it tried to chase the darkness away, the fire only pushed it toward the outer fringes of the courtyard where an angry mob gathered, shouting curses at a man crouched in their midst. The heavy scent of charcoal rose from the fire and drifted into the blackness above, as a few stragglers watched the proceeding and warmed their hands from the meager heat.

Peter pulled his robe over his face, torn between the warmth of the fire and the safety of the shadows. His eyes remained on the mob as they jostled Jesus back and forth. A crude blindfold, torn from the hem of a robe, covered his eyes. A heavy chain bound his hands behind his back as they pushed him from one angry guard to another. They spat on him as he stumbled across the rough stones, unable to gain his balance. Blood dripped freely down his chin from his split and swollen bottom lip.

Raucous laughter echoed into the darkness as a guard rushed forward and punched Jesus, sending him sprawling backward to the ground. He crashed to the stones with a dull thud, gravel biting cruelly into his cheek.

"Why don't you prophesy for us? Who hit you?"

And then the blows fell like rain, some punching, some kicking, but all laughing as he took the beating without attempting to defend himself. Nor did he cry out in pain or beg them to stop.

A growing nausea balled up in Peter's stomach as he watched the thrashing of his innocent friend.

A young woman stepped in front of Peter, peering up into his face. She nodded at the stumbling form of Jesus. "Aren't you one of his friends?"

Peter's heart shuddered and he clenched his jaw. He shook his head vehemently and tried to hold back the words that tumbled from his mouth. "No, I'm not." He pushed past the young woman and retreated to the other side of the courtyard, guilt settling in his heart like the thick black smoke that hovered in the courtyard.

A hush settled over the mob as a group of men entered the courtyard. An old man wearing priestly garments and a deep scowl led the retinue towards Jesus.

"Annas," whispered the onlookers with awe. They parted as he approached the bruised and bloody form of Jesus. "This must be serious if the former Chief Priest has come out to watch."

The old man looked down his beaked nose as a condescending smile crept over his face. "Why don't you tell us about these teachings of yours and those who call themselves your disciples?"

The air caught in Peter's throat and he pushed backward into the crowd in fear that Jesus would identify him.

Jesus lifted his swollen face and met Annas's gaze with confidence. "I've spoken openly in public. I've taught regularly in meeting places and the Temple, where the Jews gather.

Everything has been out in the open. I've said nothing in secret. So why are you treating me like a conspirator? Question those who have been listening to me. They know well what I have said. My teachings have all been truthful."

One of the guards stepped forward and drew his hand across Jesus' face with a loud crack. His head whipped to the side, blood and spit spraying the ground. "How dare you speak to the Chief Priest like that!" the guard screamed.

Jesus wiped his mouth on the shoulder of his robe and turned to face Annas again. "If I've said something wrong, prove it. But if I've spoken the truth, why this beating?"

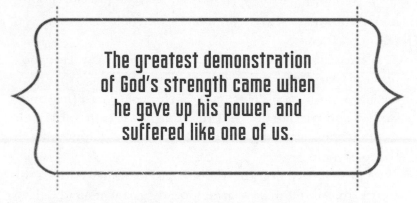

The greatest demonstration of God's strength came when he gave up his power and suffered like one of us.

Annas spit into the dirt at Jesus' feet. "Take him to Caiaphas," he said and then turned and left the courtyard.

Those gathered around the fire began to peer closer at Peter, whispering among themselves. "Aren't you one of his disciples?" one asked, poking his chest with a dirty finger.

"No," he said, averting his eyes. "I don't know what you're talking about."

"Yes, you are," one of them said as he stepped forward, anger plastered across his face. "I saw you in the garden. You're the one that cut off Malchus's ear."

"I don't know that man," he said, eyes on Jesus as the guards dragged him, still shackled, from the courtyard. As the deep black of night gave way to the murky gray of early morning, a rooster crowed in the distance and Jesus turned to look at him for the first time that night. Sorrow and brokenness etched the lines of his face with such intensity that Peter turned his face away. He ran from the courtyard, hurtling headlong into the narrow streets of Jerusalem, seeking solace in the shadows. And then Jesus' words, spoken earlier that evening, dropped like hammer-falls in his heart: *"Before the rooster crows, you will deny me three times."*

One by one the events of that terrible night settled into his mind and Peter understood for the first time all that Jesus said. Peter's own failings, his pride and over-zealous claims melted away in the light of what was happening to his Lord even now. And in that moment Peter knew that Jesus would not survive this trial. He had never intended to.

God's power is evident throughout Scripture. He created the universe, destroyed Sodom and Gomorrah, brought the plagues on Egypt, and split the Red Sea. Yet when he wanted his *love* fully revealed, he laid aside that power in favor of sacrifice. Philippians 2:6-8 says, "Though he was God, he did not think of equality with God as something to cling to. Instead, he gave up his divine privileges; he took the humble position of a slave and was born as a human being. When he appeared in human form, he humbled himself in obedience to God and died a criminal's death."

God humbled himself so much that the very ones who betrayed him put him to death. People that he created mocked him, spit on him, and tortured him. They cried out for Jesus to demonstrate his power to save himself, but he refused. He refused because *the cross would demonstrate his love, not his power.* To our world, power matters, not sacrifice.

Perhaps the greatest demonstration of God's strength came when he gave up his power and suffered like one of us. Author

Philip Yancey captures the significance of this act:

> The spectacle of the cross, the most public event of Jesus' life, reveals the vast difference between a god who proves himself through power and one who proves himself through love. Other gods, Roman gods, for example, enforced worship: in Jesus' own lifetime, some Jews were slaughtered for not bowing down to Caesar. But Jesus Christ never forced anyone to believe in him. He preferred to act by appeal, drawing people out of themselves and toward him.[1]

This should come as good news to us all, especially since low self-image seems to afflict so many of us. We are often crippled by deep internal feelings of inferiority. Our pressure-filled society places so much emphasis on external appearance, power, money and popularity that anyone who doesn't measure up in all categories feels diminished in value. Often we feel loved only when we accomplish what others expect of us. Unconditional love seems almost impossible.

Why should we feel so worthless when God went to such trouble to prove how much we matter? It's as if he said, "I love you so much that there's nothing I wouldn't do in order to know you. You matter to me. There's no limit to my love for you. I believe in you and I want to be a part of your life."

Isn't that what you really want? For someone to really love you? Not just when you do things right, but even when you screw up? God is offering that sort of love. You don't have to be the smartest, the most talented, or the most attractive. You just have to *be*.

Most of us don't find Jesus because of logical facts, but because of his loving heart, which calls to us and assures us that we are accepted. There is much historical evidence that assures our mind that the Jesus who lived two thousand years ago is indeed

God (we'll get to that later) but His *love* grips our heart and compels us to commit our lives to Him. God says, "I have loved you, my people, with an everlasting love. With unfailing love I have drawn you to myself" (Jeremiah 31:3).

Yet the death of Christ had to have a deeper meaning or it would have been merely an act of foolishness. How did his murder provide a solution to our ultimate dilemma: the fact that we can't stop sinning?

It is common for heroes to die in an effort to save those they love. The Scottish hero William Wallace died at the hands of an English king in an effort to provide freedom for his countrymen. He lived a life of great service and sacrifice and ultimately died a gruesome death. Frontiersman and legend Davy Crocket spent much of his life serving the American people. He died at the Battle of the Alamo amidst the rubble and gun smoke. And Mother Teresa spent her life caring for unwanted children in an Indian slum. Revered throughout the world for her mercy and love, even she experienced the ravages of age and death as she worked in the shadows of Calcutta. Each of these individuals did heroic things, and yet they all *died*. Only one man experienced a death that was the beginning, not the end: Christ. Unique to all of history, he was resurrected. That single divine act created an unshakeable hope for those he left behind.

The crucifixion of Christ reconnected us to God, but it was incomplete by itself. His death dealt with the problem of sin and removed our guilt, but one more step was required in order to restore us to life and enable us to experience all that God intended for us.

His death didn't address the practical problem of our addiction to sin. We still have the disease inherited from Adam embedded within our DNA. And until it's dealt with permanently, no matter how hard we try to obey God, we will continue to struggle with our addiction. Which brings us to the importance of the resurrection. When Christ rose from the dead, it completed the process of reconnecting us to God. His death removed guilt and paid the penalty for sin, but the resurrection of Christ illustrates that our death points to a new beginning. We will live forever, too.

"But," you may wonder, "how can the death and resurrection of one person pay the price and defeat death for the entire human race?" According to the apostle Paul, death entered the human race through the sins of one man, Adam. If sin entered the world through one man, then it can be defeated through the virtuous act of one man. Through his death and resurrection he offers us a new life. Jesus has not only dealt with sin, he has defeated the devil. He has effectively disabled death, destroying its power over us.

Jesus said triumphantly, "I am the resurrection and the life. Anyone who believes in me will live, even after dying. Everyone who lives in me and believes in me will never die" (John 11:25-26).

If Jesus truly rose from the dead (and a great deal of evidence supports this), then we can have confidence that we will someday rise from our own death as well.

The historical evidence of the resurrection is the very foundation of the Christian faith, not an optional part of the faith. The resurrection of Jesus Christ and Christianity as a whole stand or fall together. One cannot be true without the other. Without the historical resurrection of Jesus, the Christian faith is just another religion. Worship, Bible study, and the Church itself are worthless exercises in futility if Jesus didn't literally and physically rise from the dead. Without the resurrection we might as well toss it all away. "And if Christ has not been raised, then all our preaching is useless, and your faith is useless. And if Christ has not been raised, then your faith is useless and you are still guilty of your sins" (1 Corinthians 15:14,17).

On the other hand, if Christ *has* been raised from the dead, then he's alive at this very moment, he wants to know us personally, he forgave our sins, he has broken the power of death, and we can look forward to eternal life.

The resurrection has been the focus of the Christian faith since a few bedraggled followers huddled in a small room in Jerusalem after his crucifixion. No wonder Mary, Peter, James and John felt so devastated when they placed him in the tomb. And yet what would have happened to that small band of believers had there been no resurrection? Would they have ever found the courage to go out and impact their world? What hope would they have offered to a dying world where evil reigns? Nothing. Their words would have been hollow. Those few dogged believers in Jesus would have died, just as they lived: broken and full of sorrow.

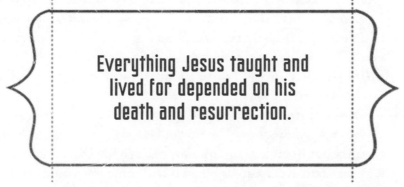

Everything Jesus taught and lived for depended on his death and resurrection.

Yet the story does not end with a dead man hanging on a Roman cross. It is humbling to know that Jesus willingly gave himself so we won't have to face our own punishment, but it is profound to know that death could not hold him. The hope he offers us today is the truth that death cannot hold us either.

Everything Jesus taught and lived for depended on his death and resurrection. All the promises and prophecies in the Bible depend on the resurrection. The entire history of God's plan to restore his relationship with mankind depends on the resurrection. The resurrection of Jesus is the single most important event in the history of the world. Your life and ours depend on it.

4

OUR GREATEST HOPES AND FEARS

Saul leaned against the carved stone pillar, relishing the scene before him. The sun dipped beneath the temple walls, casting exaggerated shadows across the courtyard. One of the Christ-followers stood in the temple courtyard, surrounded on all sides by members of the ruling council. He was young, without much of a beard, but eagerly presented his case before the leaders of Israel. The young man known as Stephen preached words from their holy book, flinging them about as if each man present did not know them by heart.

What arrogance, Saul thought. *He dooms himself with this spectacle.*

He walked amongst the crowd, keeping his distance from Stephen but never letting him out of his sight. The air crackled with an explosive tension that Saul had come to recognize with pleasure. Blood would be spilled today.

Stephen's sermon ended abruptly and he spun, taking in the crowd. His voice rose steadily, full of confidence. "You stiff-necked people, with hard hearts and clogged ears! You are just like your ancestors: You always resist God's Spirit! Was there ever a prophet your fathers did not persecute? They even killed those who predicted the coming of Jesus. And now you have betrayed and murdered him—you who have received the law but have not obeyed it."

Saul froze in mid-step, stunned with the boldness of his words. He had encountered these Christ-followers before and endured their crazy accusations, but this was too much. The crowd erupted in anger, shaking fists and spitting at him.

"You will die today, young man," Saul muttered beneath his breath, a malicious smile taking his face hostage. "I will see to it."

Yet Stephen remained calm, even as the crowd pressed against him. Instead of running or trying to protect himself, he simply lifted his eyes toward heaven. A calm settled over his face as his gaze remained fixed on the clouds. Then he said words that sealed his fate, "Look! I see heaven opening and Jesus standing at the right hand of God!"

For a brief moment, a stunned silence fell over the crowd as they tried to grasp the level of blasphemy that Stephen uttered. And then, in unison, every man covered his ears and ran forward screaming with rage. They grabbed Stephen and dragged him from the city, alternately pushing, dragging and kicking him forward.

Saul kept his distance from the mob. He did not want dirty hands or clothing after this was done. Yet he would make sure that the deed was carried out.

Just outside of the city gates was a small outcropping that overlooked the valley below. The drop was only 15 feet, but when thrown forcefully many of the stoning victims died on impact. Saul preferred the executions to remain clean and quick, but Stephen gave no indication that he would die easily. The mob hurled him over the edge but the fall didn't hurt him, and he slowly rose to his feet, facing them with confidence.

"Fine then. We'll do this the hard way," an old man with a long beard growled, taking off his robe and laying it at Saul's feet.

One by one the members of the Ruling Council did the same, until a pile of clothes was stacked neatly before Saul. They did not wish to bloody perfectly good clothing in the process of killing one Christian man.

Jewish custom allowed a mercy killing of sorts after the initial drop from a cliff. A large stone, about the size of a man's head would be dropped on the victim, usually bringing the spectacle to a quick end. If the man did not die from that blow, members of the council would then seize rocks and pelt him to death.

Saul found the process distasteful and usually chose not to participate. So he stood to the side and kept his hands clean. Yet all the while Stephen looked at him, dark brown eyes steady and unafraid. There was no crying or begging, just a deep confidence as he awaited the inevitable.

As Stephen saw the bearded man lift a large rock above his head, he turned from Saul and closed his eyes. He slowly lifted his hands, palms up, and quietly uttered, "Lord Jesus receive my spirit."

The boulder flew through the air with a whistle and landed not on his head as intended, but on his shoulder. The thud of rock and cracking of bone were audible in the still afternoon air. Stephen gasped and fell to his knees, his face contorting in pain. And then the rocks began to fall like hailstones from those gathered above him on the ledge.

Normally Saul did not watch this part of an execution, yet he could not stop himself from leaning forward. Stephen did not cover his head or try to protect himself. He simply kneeled in the dirt, face turned toward heaven. Even as the stones pounded his body, he cried out, "Lord, do not hold this sin against them!"

And then, finally, mercifully he fell silent as his body collapsed to the ground, broken and bloodied.

"Don't stop," Saul ordered. "Make sure he is dead."

Even as the men finished the execution, Saul turned away and headed back to the city, a deep contentment in his heart and a smile on his face.

Even more prevalent than the fear of public speaking is the fear of death for most people. We fear it for ourselves and we fear it for those we love. Without an eternal perspective and the confidence found in the truth of the resurrection, our mortality can terrorize us. As a society we often hide from the subject of death. Even when we do talk about death, we try to soften or disguise the harsh reality. We prefer terms such as *passed away, went to sleep,* or *went to be with the Lord.*

Yet it begs the question, "Why, exactly, do we fear death?" Most of us struggle with these six reasons:[1]

1. Death Is Mysterious and Unknown

The majority of us fear the unknown. Changing schools, heading off to college, or watching a parent leave can all bring a certain amount of apprehension because we don't know what to expect. But death poses a greater mystery than anything else; it is the greatest of all unknowns. Once having entered that realm, no one returns to tell us about it. It seems like something we can never truly understand until we experience it ourselves.

> **Without an eternal perspective and the confidence found in the truth of the resurrection, our mortality can terrorize us.**

But think of it this way: Death feels mysterious, but after the resurrection of Jesus, we know something about it that we could not have known before. It isn't permanent. Christ went through it, and he blazed a trail that we can follow. Some of the mystery has been removed because we now have footprints to follow that will lead us into new life.

2. We Have to Face Death Alone

If we could all hold hands and walk into eternity together, perhaps we could bear the idea. But we can't. We must travel alone
into that dark night.

Yet consider this: Even though it appears that we face death
alone, we now know that's an illusion. Christ will lead us through
it. The most familiar of all psalms makes the claim that we are
not alone in death: "Even though I walk through the valley of
the shadow of death, I fear no evil, for *You are with me*; Your rod
and Your staff, they comfort me" (Psalm 23:4, *NASB*, emphasis
added). Christ has actually stepped into the darkness of death
and waits to lead us safely through.

3. We Are Separated from Our Loved Ones

We wonder if our relationships can possibly continue after this
life. Will we ever meet those we love again?

We need not have this fear. Because God has conquered death
through Jesus Christ, our relationships will continue after death.
This belief does not require blind faith; it is rooted in fact. Just
as Jesus' relationship with Mary Magdalene continued after his
death (as shown in her encounter with him at the tomb), our
loving relationships will continue as well. Jesus said to the re-
pentant criminal on the cross right next to him, "I assure you, today you will be with me in paradise" (Luke 23:43). Death may
separate us temporarily from our loved ones, but the resurrection of Christ will bring us back together.

4. Our Personal Hopes and Dreams Will Not Be Realized

When we die, our goals die with us. We cannot continue to build
our dreams. Death ends the best of our plans.

Yet there is no evidence to support that theory. In fact, it is
more accurate to say that in heaven, all our hopes and dreams
will be fulfilled. C. S. Lewis suggested that being with God and
loving him is the root of all desires, that everything we long for

will have its legitimate fulfillment in our new life. Our hopes and dreams grow out of the abilities God has given us. We work toward developing them in this life. Heaven is not a place of idleness and boredom, but a place filled with responsibilities that will require our talents, abilities and creativity.

5. With Death We Cease to Exist

We fear that death could mean the end of everything. However, the truth is that life after death exists in abundance for those who die trusting in Christ. To have confidence in this truth we must examine the evidence that we exist after death. And that evidence, as we will see in the final section of this book, overwhelmingly supports Jesus' physical resurrection two thousand years ago in Jerusalem.

6. Death Is Unavoidable

Even with today's scientific advances that extend the length of our lives, all of us will die. Even Methuselah, the Old Testament patriarch who lived almost one thousand years, eventually succumbed to death. The Bible tells of a few people, like Lazarus, who were brought back from the dead, but all of them except Christ died again. No one can escape the inevitability of death.

Perhaps, but there is more to the equation. While it's true that we can't avoid the reality of death, inevitability isn't necessarily a reason to fear death. Yes, it will come, but we will go through it and come out safely in the arms of Jesus on the other side. So when it comes to death we can happily say what the apostle John said in Revelation 22:20, the most reassuring verse in the entire Bible: "Come, Lord Jesus."

Death often hits in ways we could never have anticipated. Such uncertainty feels debilitating, even for believers in Jesus. In spite of our belief, we can still wrestle with the emotional pain of death. No one expects the call in the middle of the night telling us that a loved one has died in a car wreck. We are not prepared for

CONSIDER THIS

Heaven is a real place that awaits us
after death. Each of us naturally wants
to know what we will experience in
eternity, but many of us have picked up
misguided notions along the way.
Many think of heaven as an extended,
boring, uninspiring church service. Or they
see it as a place where we will mosey
about among the clouds in long, white
gowns while strumming on harps. These
pictures are not appealing. Somehow our
image of heaven has become distorted,
and the prospect of life after death
has not captured our imaginations or
transformed our lives.

the diagnosis of cancer given to a little sister. We cannot fully comprehend the reality that death will touch each of us in a very intimate way. The Bible never promises relief from the emotionally difficult aspects of death. And anticipating heaven doesn't get rid of our apprehensions about the unknown aspects of our mortality, but it can help minimize the fear death brings by putting it in a larger context and seeing it from a new perspective. Truly understanding what the Bible says about resurrection can free us from fearing our final journey to the other side of eternity.

One of the most powerful truths of the resurrection says that heaven is a real place that awaits us after death. Death isn't the end, just the beginning. It can best be thought of as the doorway into eternal life.

But the knowledge that heaven is real and waiting for us can leave us with more questions than answers. We naturally want to know what we will experience in eternity and many of us have picked up misguided notions along the way.

Science-fiction writer Isaac Asimov expressed the attitude some have about heaven when he wrote, "I don't believe in the afterlife, so I don't have to spend my whole life fearing hell, or fearing heaven even more. For whatever the tortures of hell, I think the boredom of heaven would be even worse."[2] Sadly, a similar view of the afterlife is common among many Christians. Many think of heaven as an extended, boring, uninspiring church service. Or they see it as a place where we will mosey about among the clouds in long, white gowns while strumming on harps. These pictures of heaven are not appealing. Who wants to spend forever walking around in a choir robe bored to tears? Somehow our image of heaven has become distorted, and the prospect of life after death has not captured our imaginations or transformed our lives.

I [Sean] recently asked my students what they would do if they had only three days left to live before they died and went to heaven. How would they spend those few remaining days? Answers included skydiving, traveling, surfing, and (of course) sex. I followed up with a simple question, "So, you think there may be pleasures and experiences in this life that if you don't do them before you die, you will miss out on them altogether because they won't exist in heaven?" All but two students answered yes. The prospect of heaven dismayed and disappointed them. It simply had not captured their imaginations, and they dreaded the idea of going there. Do the rest of us believe the same thing?

Such a lack of eternal perspective sets us up for discouragement and sin. We think that if we don't experience certain pleasures now, our chance will be gone and we will never experience them. So, since God will forgive us, why not indulge? With that mindset it's no wonder so many Christians plunge into the pursuit of sex, money, drugs and popularity. We think we will find pleasure and satisfaction in these activities that will be denied us in heaven. We adopt this attitude because we carry in our minds a mistaken picture of what heaven is really like.

The donkey was a stubborn old beast, slow of body and ornery of spirit, but Saul found little fault in the creature. They were the same in many ways. He sat on its back as they walked into the sun, stirring the dust into brown clouds along the road. Behind Saul rode a small contingent of men sent by the Sanhedrin to carry out their task. The small party kept thoughts and words to themselves as they traveled the well-beaten road to Damascus.

Across the donkey's back was a leather satchel filled with parchment. Saul occasionally ran his hand across the bag and patted it happily, eager to fulfill the orders within.

It all started with Stephen, he thought, squinting in the sun. *These Christ-followers are only getting what they deserve.*

He grinned shrewdly as the memories came: standing before the Sanhedrin and basking in the praise they offered at the death of Stephen, the thrill he felt as he led a crackdown in Jerusalem to eradicate the poisonous Christ-followers from their city, and a special satisfaction at the knowledge that dozens of men and women had met their fate outside the city gates just like Stephen, while many more sat hungry and beaten in prison.

> A lack of eternal perspective sets us up for sin. We think that if we don't experience certain pleasures now, our chance will be gone and we will never experience them.

Saul nodded, relishing the power he had been given by the Ruling Council to continue the cleansing not just in Jerusalem but in Damascus as well. He raised a hand and covered his eyes as he surveyed the surroundings. They were on the outskirts of the city now. The road wandered through olive groves and green pastures dotted with white sheep. A sprinkling of small homes were scattered across the countryside, giving evidence that Damascus was near.

As the donkey plodded along, tugging at the reins and braying occasionally, beads of sweat began to build on Saul's brow. The sun was on a downward slope toward the horizon but it seemed as though the light and heat were increasing instead of fading. He wiped his forehead and turned his face to the side, trying to avoid the penetrating light.

Two things struck Saul at once: his donkey had stopped in the middle of the road, shaking with fright, and the light that beat down on him did not come from the sun. Instead of warm and yellow, it was brilliant and white. Even though he tried to turn away, the light flooded his vision, wiping away the road, the hillside and the olive groves to either side. He simply saw nothing. And then the stupid animal bolted, throwing Saul from its back. He landed on the ground with a dull thud, the air rushing from his lungs. He groped along the road, gasping for breath as he tried to stand and orient himself.

Men called out and donkeys stomped the dry earth behind him as his companions came to a halt. Yet Saul did not begin to fear until he heard the voice.

"Saul," it said, loud and commanding. "Saul, why are you persecuting me?"

He stumbled to his feet, blinking and rubbing his eyes. Yet he saw nothing but white. "Who are you?" he muttered weakly as he spun in the middle of the road.

"I am Jesus, the One you're hunting down. I want you to get up and enter the city where you will be told what to do next."

Instantly the light was gone, but his vision did not return. Instead of the blinding light, darkness settled before him, deep and impenetrable.

His companions began to scurry in the road behind him, wrestling terrified donkeys and picking up bags.

"Did you hear that?" one asked. "The voice claimed to be Jesus. But . . ." his voice trailed off.

"He's dead," another finished. "I saw him on the cross that day. There is no way that man survived. I've never seen such a scourging."

"I couldn't see anything. But I will never forget what I heard. That was Jesus talking to us."

Saul listened to their conversation, still scratching at his eyes and trying to regain his sight. "Help me!" he finally ordered, reaching his hands out before him. "I can't see."

Not knowing what else to do, they took his hand and led him the remaining distance into the city. Instead of charging in like Roman soldiers during a conquest, they quietly found a lodge and paid for a room.

For three days Saul sat in the darkness without food, water or peace. Instead he leaned against the wall, his eyes open but unseeing, and waited. His lips moved silently in prayer, uttering the words of Torah, and reciting psalms long memorized from childhood.

He drifted in and out of sleep, battling nightmares and blind desperation. On the third day, Paul lay in bed, stretched out on his back, sinking into the darkness around him. Without sight he couldn't tell whether he woke or slept. And it was in that moment the dream came, not the troubled nightmares filled with faces of persecuted Christians, but a single man with the name Ananias. In this dream the man walked into the room, placed his hands on Saul's eyes, and prayed simple words of healing. The dream was over as soon as it began and Paul woke with a start.

Some time later a sharp knock resounded on the door outside and he heard the shuffling steps of the innkeeper as he grated across the floor and unlatched the heavy wooden door. The voices were muffled but he strained to hear.

"I'm looking for Saul of Tarsus," a man said, his words shaky.

"I would think that you of all people would avoid him, Ananias."

"I don't come here willingly. I've had a vision from Jesus."

Saul leaned forward eagerly.

"Such talk could get you killed," the innkeeper hissed. "Be careful. That man is not safe."

Ananias's voice rose, insistent, "I'm telling you, Judas, he came to me in a dream and said, 'Get up and go over to Straight

Avenue. Ask at the house of Judas for a man from Tarsus. His name is Saul. He's there praying. He has just had a dream in which he saw a man named Ananias enter the house and lay hands on him so he could see again.'"

Saul gasped, suddenly feeling dizzy. "Impossible. How could this man know of my dream?"

Ananias laughed nervously outside. "And you know what I did? I argued with him. Can you believe that, Judas? I actually said to him, 'Master, you can't be serious. Everybody's talking about this man and the terrible things he's been doing, his reign of terror against your people in Jerusalem! And now he's shown up here with papers from the Chief Priest that give him license to do the same to us.' Well, Jesus put an end to that real quick. He told me not to argue and said, 'Go! I have picked him as my personal representative to Gentiles and kings and Jews. And now I'm about to show him what he's in for—the hard suffering that goes with this job.'"

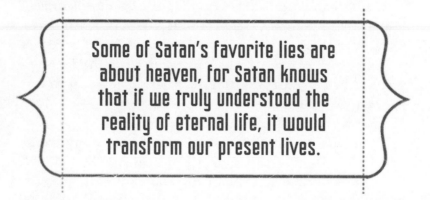

Some of Satan's favorite lies are about heaven, for Satan knows that if we truly understood the reality of eternal life, it would transform our present lives.

Judas shifted his feet and said softly, "You know, I didn't believe the rumors that this Christ person was resurrected after three days. But you make me wonder, Ananias."

"Oh, he's alive. You can believe that, Judas. And I don't know what he wants with Saul of Tarsus, but you better believe it's important, so let me in."

Saul's heart began to race as the two men shuffled outside his door. Then he heard the latch and their footsteps as they approached the bed. He recalled the looks of horror as he and his companions barged into homes in Jerusalem, terrorizing unsuspecting families and dragging them to prison in the middle of the night. And now he found himself blind and helpless before one of those very Christ-followers.

Though he dreamed that this very thing would happen, Saul wondered if Ananias had come here to kill him. Only when he felt the softness and warmth of hands on his eyes did he fully comprehend just how much he had underestimated not only Christ himself, but his followers as well.

"Brother Saul," Ananias whispered, "the Master sent me, the same Jesus you saw on your way here. He sent me so that you could see again and be filled with the Holy Spirit."

No sooner had the words left his mouth than Saul blinked and a thick yellow crust fell from his eyes. For the first time in three days he could see. He slowly rose from the bed, weak from hunger as he looked back and forth between the two men.

"I finally understand who this Jesus is," he said, finding strength in the words. "He is not dead, but alive at this very moment. I believe that he is the Messiah. Will you take me to be baptized?"

In his book *Heaven*, Randy Alcorn demonstrates that an unbiblical view of heaven has deeply infiltrated the church. In fact, he says that some of Satan's favorite lies are about heaven, for Satan knows that if we truly understood the reality of eternal life, it would radically transform our present lives.[3] If we understood what waits for us, we would have an eternal perspective from which to view the present world, and that would give us far more resolve and boldness to live godly lives here and now.

Many people believe that in heaven we will not have physical bodies. When the apostle Paul (also known as Saul of Tarsus) described our own resurrection, he said that:

> For when the trumpet sounds, those who have died will be raised to live forever. And we who are living will also be transformed. For our dying bodies must be transformed into bodies that will never die; our mortal bodies must be transformed into immortal bodies. Then, when our dying bodies have been transformed into bodies that will never die, this Scripture will be fulfilled: "Death is swallowed up in victory" (1 Corinthians 15:52-54).

Paul doesn't tell us that we will be bodiless spirits floating around. Indeed, he tells us the opposite. We will have bodies—real bodies like those we have right now. We will no longer experience the ravages of disease, age and death, and we will never die.

Have you ever wondered why the Bible speaks of a new earth as well as heaven? If we are going to heaven, why have a new earth? The book of Revelation presents the new earth as a physical place where God and his people live together. In Revelation 21, John tells of seeing a recreated earth, and then as he watches he sees the holy city of God descend to the earth. Then John says the following:

> I heard a loud shout from the throne, saying, "Look, God's home is now among his people! He will live with them, and they will be his people. God himself will be with them. He will wipe every tear from their eyes, and there will be no more death or sorrow or crying or pain. All these things are gone forever" (Revelation 21:3-4).

We rightly call this new existence "heaven" because that is what this new earth will be. But it won't look like the heaven of

Isaac Asimov, and so many of our fellow Christians.

The world we live in now offers us a glimpse of the joys and pleasures we will experience there. Randy Alcorn explains, "All our lives we've been dreaming of the New Earth. Whenever we see beauty in water, wind, flower, deer, man, woman, or child, we catch a glimpse of Heaven. Just like the Garden of Eden, the New Earth will be a place of sensory delight, breathtaking beauty, satisfying relationships, and personal joy."[4] We will not live in a sterile environment or float about among endless clouds with nothing to do. We will live on an all-new earth—just like this one, except that it will be free from storms, earthquakes, drought, floods and other disasters.

In heaven, we will experience all of our desires. Before the Fall we wanted God more than anything else, and relationship with him was the source of our greatest joy. We now struggle with evil because a malicious serpent tempted our first parents into stepping out of God's will. And from that moment on, our desires became twisted, and we used them to please ourselves.

Yet each of our desires has a legitimate satisfaction. God gave us no wrong desires. We make them unhealthy when we use them in the wrong ways. God wants to fulfill all our desires either in heaven or with himself.

Just remember this: We can't picture everything about our future existence in heaven, but we can be sure God created us to experience delight. He created the earth for our delight and pleasure. Because he loves us deeply, he wants us to experience all the pleasures he originally intended when he made us.

It is often difficult to understand a story until you reach the end. The ending brings together all the hints, clues, secrets, misunderstandings, mysteries and events that didn't seem to make sense when they happened.

God has written the story of humankind. He has taken into account the free will he gave to the characters in the story, and when Adam and Eve seemingly ruined the story on the opening page, God merely adjusted the plot and added events to bring about the good ending he originally intended. To us—the characters who find ourselves somewhere within the unresolved plot—the story may not always seem to make sense. We can't see how the chapter we're in at the moment relates to how the book ends. But the truth is, we still have an important part to play in the story.

God wants to restore a cursed and broken world to its original beauty and perfection. Every believer in Christ, regardless of his or her age, has a part to play in the restoration of our world and our society.

How will God use us to bring about this restoration? He made himself available to live within our being, giving us the power to achieve God's will on the earth. However, we are walking battlefields in which our sinful nature and God's Spirit do battle for control. That's why he gave us a group of other believers to rely on called The Church.

If ever a message should resonate with this generation, it is that we have a purpose. We aren't just here by accident. There is something we can *do* to make the world better. All of us want to be part of a story larger than ourselves.

A girl wrote a poem for me (Sean) after hearing me speak on self-image. Titled "The Mask," she says that the smiling face most people see her wear—the eyes that sparkle, the voice that sounds happy—they're only a mask. She says she's lost, confused and scared, and though she has friends, she doesn't feel like she belongs. Her final verse says that the day she feels she truly belongs will be the day she stops pretending—and stops wearing the mask.

I saw in this powerful poem the yearning to have a loving, sharing group of people that she could relate to and feel a sense of genuine belonging and acceptance. For us to survive in our faith, we must be equipped with a biblical worldview and belong to a loving community of believers who support each other and have a common mission in life. The God of restoration gave us exactly that: other believers who are there for each other and try to reach a lost world so it can know life as God intended it to be.

The story of this present world ends with our stepping into the glorious future God has waiting for us. Jesus himself promised it: "I am going there to prepare a place for you. And if I go and prepare a place for you, I will come back and take you to be with me that you also may be where I am" (John 14:2-3, *NIV*).

> **To survive in our faith, we must be equipped with a biblical worldview and belong to a loving community of believers who support each other and have a common mission.**

We should live in the reality of the completed story and not get mired down in the middle of the plot. We have been given a sneak peak on how the story ends. We don't have to live in suspense. We can live on purpose and make a difference in the lives around us. We have already won.

Many years had passed since he was referred to as Saul. These days, Jews, Gentiles and Christians simply called him Paul. He preferred it that way to tell the truth. His new name reminded him of his new life. He was no longer Saul of Tarsus, killer of Christians. He was simply Paul, Christ-follower. All these years

CONSIDER THIS

God wants to restore a cursed and broken world to its original beauty and perfection. How will God use us to bring about this restoration? He made himself available to live within our being, giving us the power to achieve God's will on the earth. However, we are walking battlefields in which our sinful nature and God's Spirit do battle for control. That's why he gave us a group of other believers to rely on called The Church. We all have a purpose. We aren't just here by accident. There is something we can do to make the world better. All of us want to be part of a story larger than ourselves.

later the irony did not escape him and he often found himself smiling at the mercy and humor in God's plan.

It was in such a mood that Paul found himself that day in Athens as he stood on top of Mars Hill. The city sprawled below him like a vine, twisting and curling across the countryside, filled with life and beauty.

Instead of taking his usual stroll through the city that morning, he purposefully walked toward the Areopagus, a large rock that jutted out from the side of the hill. Although it had served many purposes throughout history, these days the giant stone outcropping was a gathering place for Epicurean and Stoic philosophers to debate theories on the gods. They invited Paul to discuss his ideas after a heated debate the day before.

They waited for him eagerly, almost casually, as he limped slowly onto the rough stone surface that overlooked the Acropolis just a few miles away.

"So, stranger," they enticed, getting right to the point, "you have us baffled. We've never heard any ideas like yours before. Explain them to us so we can understand."

So Paul stood in the open space at the Areopagus and laid it out for them. "It is plain to see that you Athenians take your religion seriously. When I arrived here the other day, I was fascinated with all of the shrines I came across. And then I found one inscribed to the Unknown God. I'm here to introduce you to this God so that you can worship intelligently and know who you're dealing with."

They listened patiently as he continued. "The God who made the world and everything in it, this Master of sky and land, doesn't live in custom-made shrines or need the human race to run errands for him, as if he couldn't take care of himself. He makes the creatures; the creatures don't make him. Starting from scratch, he made the entire human race and made the earth as well, with plenty of time and space for living so we could seek after God, and not just grope around in the dark but actually find him. He doesn't play hide-and-seek with us. He's not remote; he's near. We live and move in him, can't get away from him! One of your poets said it well: 'We're the God-created.' Well, if we are the God-created, it doesn't make a lot of sense to think we could hire a sculptor to chisel a god out of stone for us, does it? God overlooks it as long as you don't know any better—but that time has passed. The unknown is now known, and he's calling for a radical life-change. He has set a day when the entire human race will be judged and everything set right. And he has already appointed the judge, confirming him before everyone by raising Jesus from the dead."

As soon as the Epicureans and the Stoics heard Paul say that Jesus had been raised from the dead, they began to laugh and wander away, cracking jokes about the crazy Jew. And yet Paul did not call them back or try to argue.

"Let's do this again. I want to hear more," a Greek scholar said to his companions as they walked down the hill. He turned to look at Paul one last time and nodded politely as he jogged after his friends.

Paul watched the crowd disappear and took a deep breath. "So it goes in Athens," he muttered, as he too wandered away. "May some of them remember, Lord. May some of them come to know you."

"Excuse me," a woman said, tapping Paul on the shoulder.

He turned to find a young woman with curious eyes and a bright smile. "My name is Damaris and I was listening to you debate with my friend Dionysius. We want to hear more."

"I would love to tell you," Paul said, closing his eyes and offering a silent prayer of thanks.

When missionaries enter a new culture, they study that culture, listen to the people, and try to understand their values. They spend time getting to know individuals and building relational bridges. They ask questions such as, "What do they believe?" "How do they think?" "What do they know about Christianity?" Missionaries do not adopt the foreign culture, but seek to understand the people in order to find an opening for the gospel.

> Jesus calls us to be his hands and feet to love others. He wants us to go out into the world and have conversations with people who don't know him.

We don't need to create an inward-focused Christian subculture, but we should be the salt and light to our world. Salt makes food more enticing, and light attracts people. Jesus calls us to be his hands and feet to love others. He wants us to do exactly what the apostle Paul did: go out into the world and have conversations with people who don't know him.

Most people you know probably have a very negative perception of the church. In his eye-opening book *They Like Jesus but Not the Church*, pastor Dan Kimball lists six common perceptions our generation has of the Christian church:

1. The church is an organized religion with a political agenda.
2. The church is judgmental and negative.
3. The church is dominated by males and oppresses females.
4. The church is homophobic.
5. The church arrogantly claims all religions are wrong.

6. The church is full of fundamentalists who take the whole Bible literally.[5]

David Kinnaman, president of the Barna Research Group, came to similar conclusions in his recent book *unChristian*. Non-Christians were asked to describe whether they think churches are loving environments where they feel accepted regardless of how they look or what they do. Sadly, only one in five viewed Christians this way. He says, "Only a small percentage of outsiders strongly believe that the labels 'respect, love, hope, and trust' describe Christianity."[6]

How sad that is what the world thinks of us. But how do we go about changing a deeply held belief? As always these misperceptions are best overcome through relationships. Paul changed his world by creating friendships with people that didn't know Jesus. If we as Christians don't build genuine friendships with nonbelievers, they will never know what Christians are like.

The world is a mission field, and God has called us to be his personal ambassadors to it. We should tell people, as Paul did, that Jesus has risen from the dead and offers everyone a new life. But we shouldn't just preach this truth; we should live out Christ's example of sacrificial love to each other and to the outside world.

We cannot shout this message from a distance. Rather, we must speak it up close and personal. We should follow the example of Jesus, who was known as a friend of tax collectors and sinners, and build relationships with people who feel estranged from the church. Jesus did not merely announce the kingdom of God; he demonstrated its reality by feeding the poor, healing the sick, and ministering to the outcasts.

On a personal level you can look at it this way: Who in your life doesn't fit in? Befriend that person. Make a difference in that life. And then do it again. And again. Live where you are, on purpose.

For the early church, belief in the resurrection meant more than merely looking forward to the end of the story. Rather, their belief in the resurrection caused them to participate in advancing the plot, to participate in God's restoration by claiming the present world for his kingdom. Even though they were small in number, they trusted in a powerful God. They claimed the world for God through both action and belief. If we are going to be faithful to Jesus, how can we do any less?

I [Sean] had a student come to me torn over his addiction to Internet pornography. He was deeply embarrassed at his inability to control himself. Visibly shaking, he looked me in the eyes and said, "I can control every area of my life but this one. I am so ashamed." I encouraged him to embrace God's grace and to realize that he didn't have to struggle with this on his own—in fact, he couldn't. The resurrection of Christ demonstrated that no sin is too terrible to be forgiven. If God is big enough to forgive Paul for murdering Christian men and women, he is big enough to forgive anything.

Of course, being freed from our guilt doesn't mean that we no longer have to follow God's commands. Accepting what Christ has done for us should drive us to desire obedience rather than rebellion. When we come to terms with the significance of what Christ did for us on the cross, it changes our lives. And a grateful heart seeks to please, not to hurt or hide.

Old bodies rot in prison long before death actually comes to claim them. A wry smile twisted the corners of Paul's mouth as he looked at the emaciated legs sticking out from beneath his robe. None would argue that he'd ever been much to look at, but now, at the end of his life, there was simply nothing left to see. Pale skin hung from brittle bones. What little hair he had left clumped together on his mostly bald scalp. His eyes were sunken and his teeth missing. His mangy and threadbare robe constantly threatened to fall to the ground for lack of meat on his bones.

And yet, sitting thirty feet below the ground in a damp, bug infested Roman prison, Paul felt more alive than at any point in his life. This body that wrapped him in age and disease would soon be stripped away and he would no longer struggle with the trappings of a mortal frame. Death was just a short distance away, and with it would come life.

The notoriety of Nero's prison was recognized throughout the world. Little more than a holding cell for those who would die at the hands of gladiators or be fed to lions, it became a fearsome place for most who found themselves trapped within. Finding oneself in the light of day usually meant a short trip to the Coliseum and a grisly death before the mob.

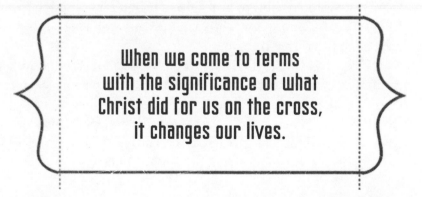

When we come to terms with the significance of what Christ did for us on the cross, it changes our lives.

And so Paul waited, hungry and alone. His only comfort were the letters he wrote to those he'd met on his travels, men and women trying to live out lives committed to Christ. Friends and disciples would collect the letters and transport them for him, often replacing the scrolls with new pen and parchment.

Yet for some reason he did not reach for the paper in his cell and begin a new epistle. Just yesterday he'd sent his dear friend Timothy another letter, and with it gone he found himself at a lack for words. This was a day to be still.

"For what do I listen, Lord?" he spoke eagerly into the empty cell. "Will this be the day you take me home?"

Just the thought settled Paul's heart. "Home," he muttered again, his mind not on the distant town of Tarsus, but the heaven he waited for. He nodded slowly, eyes squeezed shut as he tried to picture in his finite mind what glories waited for him beyond the veil of death. "Yes, Lord, let this be the day."

He was aware of falling asleep but he woke some time later to the sound of iron bars grating across stone. Before he could open his eyes to see who entered his cell, rough hands grabbed his arms and lifted him off the ground like a child's doll. Without a word the two soldiers dragged him from the prison.

I wonder what it will be? he thought, taking a deep breath and preparing himself. *Food for the lions? Target practice for the Gladiators? Perhaps even a human torch at the whim of Nero? It matters not. This end will just be the beginning.*

Yet the guards did not take Paul to the Coliseum. Instead he was taken outside the city by the rear gates and led to the Roman military encampment.

"*Capitis Amputatio*," one of the guards yelled, attracting the attention of a large man who stood in the center of a large pit.

Capital amputation. Beheading. Such mercy for me, Lord? A quick death when I brought such pain on others in my life? You give me far better than I deserve.

Paul lifted his eyes and beheld a swath of seamless blue sky. He smiled.

The guards threw him into the pit and shackled his frail legs to the large wooden block that sat in the middle of the dugout.

"Strip and scourge him," they ordered the executioner and then turned back to the prison without another glance at Paul.

Without a word the executioner stripped the filthy robes from his body and surveyed the sagging skin and protruding bones with distaste. Not a man given to mercy, even he could see there was little use in whipping this old man. Yet he did as he was told.

In the final moments of his life, Paul thought of those who had gone on before. He remembered the look on Stephen's face as he boldly stood before those who accused him of heresy. He thought of the men and women he'd ordered killed. He thought of the children he had orphaned. But more than anything, as the rod fell across his back time and again, he thought of a man named Jesus who endured this much and more for his sake so that he would know life after death.

Paul did not cry out. He did not struggle. He simply laid across the wooden block and waited. Within a few moments the executioner gave up, deriving no pleasure from this particular task. Paul heard him draw the sword from the scabbard at his side. He braved one more glance at a perfect blue sky and smiled as the Roman sword whistled through the air.

We often fulfill the mission of restoring a lost world to Jesus most effectively when we endure times of crisis or suffering. Most of us can exhibit love, joy, peace and patience when life is good. But how many people display gratitude, courage and optimism in the midst of a storm? When tragedy strikes, when we're hurting or mistreated and still have joy, people sit up and take notice. While rotting in a Roman prison, the apostle Paul wrote letters of hope and encouragement to his friends. Fourteen of those letters were so treasured by the early church that they became books in the Bible. Paul used his time of suffering for a purpose.

As believers in Jesus Christ, we should extend God's grace to others and be living examples of Christ's love and forgiveness.

Our world needs to see the length that Jesus went to reconcile us to God. Our task is to help people move from focusing on their mistakes to embracing God's love and forgiveness.

God takes forgiveness very seriously. Jesus said, "If you forgive those who sin against you, your heavenly Father will forgive you. But if you refuse to forgive others, your Father will not forgive your sins" (Matthew 6:14-15). We can't withhold forgiveness from others and walk in relationship to God. Yet if we have not first grasped God's forgiveness to us, we can't truly offer it to others.

We live in an age marked largely by isolation, emptiness and hurt. There are two primary causes of the aloneness many feel today: technology and fatherlessness. Our age has seen unprecedented technological advances, which have benefited our world greatly. But sadly, these same inventions have caused much loneliness, disconnecting us from God and each other. People spend far more time on their computers, listening to music, playing video games, and surfing the Internet than they do face to face. In *Generation Me,* Dr. Jean Twenge notes that because of technology, "we're malnourished from eating a junk-food diet of instant messages, e-mail, and phone calls, rather than the healthy food of live, in-person interaction."[7]

The deepest source of loneliness, however, is fatherlessness. The greatest problem in the world today isn't the threat of terrorism, unbridled violence, or global poverty. The greatest problem facing our world is the lack of loving fathers involved in the lives of their kids. Children with absent or neglectful fathers grow up lacking the deep, overarching love every person craves.

According to *Divorce Magazine,* "Fatherless homes account for 63 percent of youth suicides, 90 percent of homeless/runaway children, 85 percent of children with behavior problems, 71 percent of high school dropouts, 85 percent of youths in prison and well over 50 percent of teen mothers. The number of single-parent homes has skyrocketed, displacing many children in this country. Approximately 30 percent of U.S. families are now being headed by a single parent. In 80 percent of those families, the mother is the sole parent. The United States is the world's leader in fatherless families."[8]

Our culture is falling apart at the seams because there are so few fathers holding it together. Many of us know what it feels like to live in a home with just one parent. Those lucky enough to have both at home can still feel the sting of uninvolved fathers. It's an epidemic in our culture. Yet we must remember that God calls himself Father and wants us to know him as such. That is why his love can't just be known in our homes and our churches. We must take it to the world.

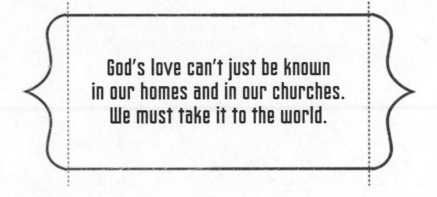

God's love can't just be known
in our homes and in our churches.
We must take it to the world.

Biblical faith is always translated into loving and serving those around us. Jesus demonstrated such love through his life. He touched the untouchables, loved the unlovable, and approached the unapproachable. He wept over evil, responded with anger at injustice, and always had time for those who were neglected. He saw beyond external appearances and loved people in a manner fitting their true needs. Jesus called us to love our enemies, bless those who persecute us, and ultimately overcome the world through the kind of love he showed to us on the cross.

As a follower of Christ, the apostle Paul tried to do the same thing. All these years later we can see what an impact he made on his world. Is it possible that God wants to use us as well? The resurrection of Christ can speak loudly to the world through our lives.

THE EVENT THAT CHANGED HISTORY

It was a random decision but one that would haunt Thomas for days; he went for a walk that Sunday morning. He rose early, long before the others, and slipped into the crisp morning air. He began walking without a destination, and found himself some hours later on the side of a hill watching the sun rise over Jerusalem. Just a week earlier he watched Jesus enter the city like a conquering hero, and now he lay buried in a stone tomb.

As the hours passed Thomas picked his sorrows, like splinters in a festering wound. His stomach rumbled with hunger and his legs grew numb as he sat on the cold stone, and yet he did not move. With each confession of disappointment, the tears came anew and he sank further into despair.

"It wasn't supposed to be like this," Thomas moaned, burying his face in his arms and allowing the heaving sobs to wrack his body. He wept until the tears were spent and his eyes were bloodshot. As the sun began to set, he pulled himself from the ground and wandered back to the city, feet dragging and heart heavy. Night had fallen over the streets of Jerusalem like a thick blanket by the time he passed through the gates. Yet there was an electricity in the air, people whispered in doorways but did not look one another in the eye, and the Roman guards scurried along the cobblestone streets with greater purpose than usual.

So it begins, he thought. *Soon they will round up the rest of us and we will most likely die as Jesus did.*

"I have nothing left to live for," he muttered as he approached Peter's house. He reached for the door latch and paused, listening to the excited whispers within.

He tried to pull the door open but it was locked. "That's odd," he said, yanking at the door in frustration. "Peter never locks his door." Then he noticed that all the windows were drawn shut as well. Thomas leaned against the wall and rapped his knuckles against the old splintered wood.

A few seconds later the heavy door swung outwards and revealed the towering form of Peter. Thomas slipped past him, eyes on the floor.

Peter's strong hands gripped his shoulders, the fingers digging into his flesh. "Thomas!" he bellowed. "We have seen the Master. Jesus is alive!"

Thomas looked around the room for the first time and saw his friends. No longer were they the bedraggled group of Christ-followers that laid a dead man in a tomb. Something had come over them, something Thomas could not explain.

He opened his mouth but no words came. He was tempted to argue but the look on Peter's face suggested there was no lie in his words. And yet Thomas could not believe. He pulled away from Peter, his heart battling with reality and hope. "Unless I see the nail holes in his hands, put my finger in the nail holes, and stick my hand in his side, I won't believe it."

He spoke those words to Peter eight days ago and even now he could not bring himself to believe his friends. Their story had not changed. They said Jesus was alive. They said they had seen him and talked to him and embraced him. Yet Thomas knew that dead men don't come back. He wanted it to be true. Hoped it was true. But it made no sense. He had no proof but the word of his friends.

So they sat in Peter's house on Sunday night, breaking bread around a low table. He looked from one face to the next, studying their zeal, waiting to find deceit. Nothing. These men and women he'd spent the last three years with *believed* that Jesus was no longer dead.

I want to believe too, Lord. I want to believe . . . Thomas thought as he slowly chewed a piece of bread. He stirred the half-eaten plate of food before him, trying to muster an appetite that wasn't there. He did not notice the room grow suddenly quiet or see that all eyes were on the wall behind him. Instead he wrestled with his own thoughts, his own disbelief.

And then a voice, so gentle, so familiar, spoke behind him, and the hair on Thomas's arms stood on end.

"Peace to you," it said.

His heart leapt in his chest and he sat up slowly, afraid to turn, afraid that the voice was a conjuring of his own imagination. Hesitantly Thomas rose and lifted fearful eyes to the face of a risen Christ.

The smile Jesus offered Thomas was full of love and compassion. He reached out his hands, palms upward, exposing the holes in his wrists where cruel steel spikes had pinned him to his cross. "Take your finger and examine my hands, Thomas. Take your hand and stick it in my side. Believe," he said, speaking right to the heart of Thomas's doubt.

Every eye in the room was fixed on Thomas as he reached out to touch his Lord with shaking hands. The wounds were real and so was the man that stood before him. "My Master! My God!" Thomas gasped, falling to his knees before Jesus and throwing his arms around him.

Belief welled in the heart of Thomas even as Jesus spoke, "So, you believe because you've seen with your own eyes. Even better blessings are in store for those who believe without seeing."

Whatever your opinion about Jesus and the resurrection, everyone has to admit that something significant happened on that first Easter morning—significant enough to alter the course of history, even to the point of changing the calendar from B.C. (before Christ) to A.D. (the Latin *Anno Domini*—the year of our Lord).

That "something" was so dramatic that it completely changed the lives of eleven men, enabling them to endure abuse, suffering, and even death. Only an empty tomb could accomplish such a thing. Reports of the resurrection of Jesus Christ have shaken the foundations of thought and shaped the course of history from that time forward. Obviously, something happened. Something big.

Two thousand years later you and I find ourselves in an interesting position. We know that a dramatic event unfolded, but we are left with many questions regarding the details. And that's okay. Just as Thomas needed proof, needed to touch the holes in Jesus' hands, we too have the right to question and wonder. God does not expect us to go on blind faith. He wants us to discover the truth.

> ## Just as Thomas needed proof, we too have the right to question and wonder. God does not expect us to go on blind faith. He wants us to discover the truth.

But even that word, "truth," creates a problem. Isn't truth a fluid concept in our culture? Some would make the argument that what is true for one is not true for all. How then can we know the facts about what happened on that Easter morning so long ago?

I (Sean) once performed the following experiment with my students. I placed a jar of marbles in front of them and asked, "How many marbles are in the jar?"

They responded with different guesses, 221, 168, and so on. Then after giving them the correct number of 188, I asked, "Which of you is closest to being right?"

They all agreed that 168 was the closest guess. And they all agreed that the number of marbles was a matter of objective fact, not one determined by personal preference.

Then I passed out *Starburst* candies to each student and asked, "Which flavor is right?" They all thought this was a ridiculous question because each person had a preference that was right for them.

"That's correct," I concluded. "The right flavor has to do with a person's preferences. It is a matter of personal opinion, not objective fact."

Then I asked, "Are religious claims like the number of marbles in a jar, or are they a matter of opinion, like one's candy preference?" Most students concluded that religious claims belonged in the category of candy preference. We then discussed the claims of Christianity. I pointed out that the claims of Christianity are based on historical fact—the resurrection of Jesus. I reminded them that while many people may reject the historical resurrection of Jesus, it is not the type of claim that can be "true for you, but not true for me." The tomb was either empty on the third day, or it held a body—there is no middle ground. Before we can grasp the power of the resurrection of Jesus, we must realize that we are dealing with a matter of *fact,* not opinion.

If we insist on evidence when we approach the daily decisions of our lives, why should we discard these tools when it comes to our religious convictions? We should never accept religious beliefs on "blind faith," but on credible evidence.

In light of that, we must ask ourselves a few questions: Did Jesus really live? Did he die as the Bible says? Was he supernaturally resurrected two thousand years ago as Christians claim? And, most importantly, is Jesus worth trusting with my present life and eternal destiny?

Mary wanted to run. Every fiber in her being screamed that she should turn from the sight and flee, find a safe place and let herself cry. But she would not turn away from Jesus in this moment, not with him so near, not with his eyes upon her. Had he not stayed by her side when the city leaders brought her to him and demanded that she be stoned for sleeping with a married man? Yes he had stayed, and even ordered that any man in the crowd who did not sin could hurl the first rock at her. One by one her accusers slipped away and she stood before Jesus, shame eating her alive. He was the only person in her life who had not abandoned her and she would not turn from him now, even as he hung on a cross ten feet above her, the life draining from his body.

Mary sat with Jesus' mother and John a short distance away, keeping vigil and trying not to hear the derisive curses that on-lookers hurled at Jesus as they watched the spectacle.

"You bragged that you could tear down the Temple and then rebuild it in three days—so show us your stuff! Save yourself! If you're really God's Son, come down from that cross!"

"Don't you know what the Scriptures say? Cursed is he who hangs on a tree!"

Laughter filled the air even as heavy clouds settled lower in the sky. Mary could sense no rain in the air, just a darkness that matched the mood in her heart. Those gathered on the hillside were uneasy and began to drift away. The clouds began rolling in at noon, and now, three hours later, the sky was heavy with darkness.

"Why don't they just leave?" John whispered as he cast a ten-tative glance at Caiaphas and the other priests. "They got what they wanted. Why don't they just leave us alone to grieve?"

Mary shook her head. She knew these men. "They want to see it finished. They want the satisfaction of *watching* him die."

Caiaphas let out a pleased chuckle and stood before Jesus, arms crossed. "He saved others—he can't save himself! King of Israel, is he? Then let him get down from that cross. We'll all become believers then! He was so sure of God—well, let him rescue his 'Son' now—if he wants him! He did claim to be God's Son, didn't he?"

"Fools!" John hissed beneath his breath. "Like they will ever understand what Jesus meant."

Jesus did not answer their ridicule, did not even look at them. But an agonized groan rose in his chest as words spilled from his mouth. "My God, my God, why have you abandoned me?"

Mary gasped, choking back the tears, as she buried her face in John's shoulder.

"He's calling for Elijah," one of the bystanders laughed.

"Let's see if Elijah comes and saves him now," another said.

Mary could not look on his wounds, the bloody lash marks or the steel spikes driven into his wrists and ankles, but she did find his face and she let herself suffer with him. He blinked heavily, eyes rolling back in his head. The hours had passed slowly and though she did not want her Lord to die neither did she want him to suffer. It was with intense agony and deep relief that she realized the end was near.

And then Jesus opened his eyes, the lids hanging heavy. "I am thirsty," he whispered, his tongue thick and voice slurred.

One of the onlookers ran toward the hillside and broke a long stick from a hyssop bush. He grabbed a sponge and dipped it in a clay jar holding wine vinegar and then raised the branch to Jesus' mouth.

Then he did something that Mary would never forget; Jesus pushed up with his legs one last time, his face contorted in pain. He took a deep breath, lifted his eyes, and said, "It is finished!" His voice carried with such force that everyone who stood on the rocky hillside of Golgotha turned to look at him. Then his body fell limp and his head rolled forward. He neither breathed nor spoke again.

No sooner had the words left his mouth than a deep rumbling rose from the ground beneath them and the entire hillside started to shake. The ground split in places, tearing into the rock like warm bread.

Panic stricken, Caiaphas and his fellow priests turned and ran down the hillside. The captain of the guard and the soldiers that were with him looked at one another in fright as they tried to steady themselves.

"This has to be the Son of God," the captain muttered, dropping his spear and staring at the limp form of Jesus.

Mary turned to John. "What do we do now?"

"We wait for Joseph of Arimathea. He has gone to Pilate to ask for the body. Then we must hurry to dress it. Sabbath begins at sundown."

"That isn't what I meant," she said softly, fresh tears running down her face and leaving muddy rivulets on her face. "What do we do *now*?"

John wiped a sleeve across his eyes, wiping his own tears away. "I don't know," he whispered. "This changes everything."

Crucial Facts About Christ's Crucifixion

Before looking into Christ's resurrection, we must first look at the events leading up to it. These events set the stage and provide valuable information about the resurrection itself. Understanding the historical fact of his death is fundamental to our conviction about his resurrection.

The Trials of Jesus

After his betrayal and arrest, Jesus went through six different trial cross-examinations before facing crucifixion. One was before Annas, the elder high priest; another was before Caiaphas, the Roman appointed priest; the third was before the Jewish council, the Sanhedrin; the fourth was before the Roman governor, Pontius Pilate; the fifth before Herod; and the sixth was again before Pilate. In total, there were three Jewish trials and three Roman trials.

Why all this concern over one man? Both the Roman and Jewish authorities had various concerns about Christ's remaining at large. N. T. Wright gives five compelling reasons why the Jewish authorities wanted him executed:[1]

1. Many of the Jewish leaders considered Jesus to be a "false prophet" who was leading people astray.

2. Jesus claimed authority over the greatest Jewish symbol: the Temple. The Temple was the center of Jewish national life as well as being considered the place of God's presence. Jesus claimed to personally replace the role the Temple had played in the religious life of the Jews.

3. Jesus saw himself as the Messiah, which meant he could potentially become the focus of serious revolutionary activity.

4. They saw Jesus as a political risk, whose actions might provoke the wrath of Rome upon the nation.

5. Finally, at the climax of the hearing, Jesus pleaded guilty to the above charges, and then he also made blasphemous claims placing himself alongside the God of Israel.

James Montgomery Boice narrows the charges down to one central reason why the Jewish authorities sought Jesus' death:

No less than six separate charges had been brought against him. First, he had been charged with threatening to destroy the Jewish temple (Matthew 26:61). Second, he was accused of being an evildoer (John 18:30). Third, he was charged with perverting the nation (Luke 23:2). Fourth, it was said that he had forbidden Jews to pay taxes to Caesar (Luke 23:2). Fifth, he was said to have stirred up the people (Luke 23:5). Sixth, he was cited for having made himself a king (Luke 23:2). Here were six serious accusations. But these charges were not the real reason for the hatred of the Jewish leaders for Jesus or their prosecution of the case against him before Pilate. The real accusation is that he had claimed to be the unique Son of God, which they judged blasphemy.[2]

According to Jewish law, crucifixion was an appropriate punishment for the charge of blasphemy.

While the Jews were concerned with the religious implications of Jesus' actions, the Romans were far more concerned with politics, economics, and the authority of Rome. They crucified him as a rebel against Rome. When Jesus replied to the governor's question, "Are you the King of the Jews?" by saying, "It is as you say," he gave them grounds for execution. To say that Jesus was king was to imply that Caesar was not.

Justice Haim Cohn, while a member of the Supreme Court of Israel, wrote an article titled "Reflections on the Trial of Jesus." He said, "There can be no doubt that a confession such as this was sufficient in Roman law for conviction of the defendant."[3] The offense was punishable with death, and Pontius Pilate was vested with the right to pass the death sentence.

Dr. Craig A. Evans, Distinguished Professor of New Testament at Acadia Divinity College of Acadia University, sums up the reasons for Jesus' crucifixion: "Jesus provided the grounds for a sentence of death from both the Jewish authorities (i.e., capital blasphemy) and the Roman authorities (i.e., treason and sedition)."[4] In their eyes Jesus had to die because he was a dangerous troublemaker and a heretic.

> When Jesus replied to the governor's question, "Are you the King of the Jews?" by saying, "It is as you say," he was giving his Roman accusers grounds for his execution.

Pontius Pilate

Jesus was accused of treason by Jewish religious rulers and brought for trial before the Roman governor, Pontius Pilate. For years the only historical evidence for Pilate's existence was literary, and some historians doubted his existence.[5] But in 1961 two Italian archaeologists excavated the Mediterranean port city of Caesarea that served as the Roman capital of Palestine. They uncovered a two-by-three-foot inscription in Latin that reads: "Pontius Pilate, Prefect of Judea." This archaeological discovery of a historical reference to Pilate confirmed his existence and his position.

All available evidence shows Pilate to have been an extremely cruel and merciless ruler. He was responsible for countless atrocities and numerous executions without a trial. He washed his hands to avoid responsibility in the death of Christ. Pilate wanted to set Jesus free, not because he thought him to be innocent, but to irritate the chief priests.

Finally, after three Jewish trials and three Roman trials, the Jewish authorities, in conjunction with the Roman authorities, nailed him to a cross and hung him up to die. At this point, various "security precautions" were taken to make sure that Jesus was truly dead.

It was nearly four o'clock in the afternoon when Joseph found himself standing before Pontius Pilate. He'd seen the man throughout the city, but never had he been in his presence, or wanted to be for that matter.

"Thank you for granting me an audience, Governor," Joseph said, bowing his head and studying the mosaic tile floor at his feet.

Pilate studied him in silence for several moments. "You are a member of the Sanhedrin, are you not?"

"Yes, sir," Joseph said, raising his head and looking at Pilate for the first time.

The Roman despot looked as one would expect a servant of Caesar to look: cold, arrogant and disinterested. His hair was cropped close to the scalp and his face was clean shaven. A large nose, dark eyes, and olive skin attested to his Roman heritage.

"And you are a rich man?" Pilate asked.

Again Joseph nodded. "I have been blessed with many olive groves and a large family, Governor. I am indeed a rich man."

"Then what would you need with me? It does not appear as though you lack for anything."

Joseph took a deep breath and tried to calm his racing heart. "I have come to ask you for the body of Jesus of Nazareth." He stated his request simply and let the words fall into hostile air.

Pilate looked up, taking a sudden interest. "Is he dead already? It has only been a few hours."

"Yes, Governor. He breathed his last just a short time ago."

"Is that so?" Pilate motioned one of his soldiers forward. "Bacchus, go see if this man Jesus is indeed dead. And verify with any of the Roman guards present that there is no life in his body."

The soldier nodded assent and jogged from the room, his sandals clapping against the stone.

Pilate nodded at Joseph. "You can wait."

"Thank you, Governor."

"Don't thank me yet. I have granted you nothing." Then a curious expression crossed his face and he asked, "Why would a man such as you, so powerful and well respected with Caiaphas and that lot, want the body of a condemned criminal?"

Joseph pursed his lips and swallowed. He would not cry before Pontius Pilate. "He was my friend," he said simply.

Pilate grunted but said nothing else until Bacchus returned thirty minutes later.

"It is true," the captain said as he stood at attention before Pilate. "The man they call Jesus has died."

"Very well then," Pilate said, waving Joseph out of his presence. "You may have the corpse. Do with it what you will."

"There is one other thing, Governor," Bacchus said as Joseph slipped from the room. "Caiaphas requests an audience with you tonight."

Joseph jogged down the marble steps just as Pilate began to curse.

By the time he reached the hillside, the Roman guards had taken the body of Jesus and laid him flat on the ground. John, the mother of Jesus, and Mary stood by the body, weeping loudly.

"We must do this quickly," Joseph whispered. "It will be sundown shortly and the law forbids us to prepare a body on the Sabbath."

"But we have nothing with which to dress the body," John said.

Joseph smiled sadly. "You need not worry about that. I have prepared everything."

The two men lifted his body carefully and laid it on a linen cloth that Mary spread across the ground. And then as gently as they could, the small group of mourners carried his body to the tomb.

Death by Crucifixion

The Jews were well aware that Jesus had predicted his own resurrection. Fearing that his followers might make it appear that Jesus had risen from the dead, they were equally cautious to make sure he was dead and remained dead. The first of these precautions was death by crucifixion. The death would be public, brutal, and certain.

The History of Crucifixion

All four Gospels tell of Jesus' death by crucifixion (see Mark 15:27-37; Matthew 27:35-50; Luke 23:33-46; John 19:23-30). While they do not describe the process in detail, much can be discovered about the nature of crucifixion through historical, literary and archaeological evidence.

Crucifixion was a very common method of execution during the time of Christ. In fact, evidence indicates that crucifixion was done in Athens as early as seven hundred years before Christ was born.

The Brutality of Crucifixion

Crucifixion was the most dreadful form of punishment. Victims were tortured so severely that sometimes the Romans even felt pity for them.

Those unfortunate enough to witness the horrors of a crucifixion reported the most wretched sort of death. Flavius Josephus says that when the Romans threatened to crucify one of the Jewish prisoners, the entire garrison surrendered in order to obtain safe passage. Crucifixion was so gruesome and degrading that the Romans usually excluded Roman citizens and reserved it for slaves or rebels to discourage uprisings. It was used primarily in political cases. During the Roman Empire, crucifixion was widely considered the worst possible way to die.

"The pain was absolutely unbearable," observes Alexander Metherell, MD, PhD. "In fact, it was literally beyond words to describe; they had to invent a new word: *excruciating*. Literally, *excruciating* means 'out of the cross.' Think of that: they needed to create a new word, because there was nothing in the language that could describe the intense anguish caused during crucifixion."[6]

The Custom of Whipping

After the verdict of crucifixion came down from those in charge, soldiers tied the victim to a post outside the court. The criminal was stripped of his clothes and then severely flogged by soldiers. The Gospels record that Jesus was whipped in such a way before his crucifixion.

The whip was known as a flagrum and had a heavy wooden handle that attached to leather strips of varying lengths. Sharp, jagged pieces of bone and metal were woven into the strips to cause additional damage when it struck the victim. Roman soldiers would repeatedly strike a victim's back without mercy, causing the iron balls to tear deeply into the skin and muscle until all that was left were ribbons of bleeding flesh. If left unattended, these wounds could easily kill a person within a few hours.

Jewish law limited the punishment to forty lashes. The Pharisees, with their rigid religious observance, would limit their lashes to thirty-nine, so that if they miscounted they would not break the law. The Romans, on the other hand, had no such limitations. Out of disgust or anger, they could ignore the Jewish limitation, and probably did so in the case of Jesus.

In the *Martyrdom of Polycarp*, we read, "For even when they [the Christians] were so torn by whips that the internal structure of their flesh was visible as far as the inner veins and arteries, they endured so patiently that even the bystanders had pity and wept."[7] The body was swollen, bloody, and disfigured. It was the custom after this torture to mock the victim, and the Roman soldiers did this to Christ. They placed a purple robe around his shoulders and a "crown of thorns" on his head to mock his claims of royalty.

The Crown of Thorns

We don't know what type of thorn was used as a mock crown for Jesus. One possibility is a plant now called the Syrian Christ-thorn, a shrub about twelve inches high with two large, sharp, curved thorns at the bottom of each leaf. This plant is common in Palestine, especially around the site of Golgotha where Christ was crucified.

Another plant, simply called the Christ-thorn, is a dwarf-sized shrub four to eight feet high. The branches can be bent easily to form a crown, and the thorns, in pairs of different lengths, are stiff like nails or spikes.

The thorns of either plant, when pressed into the scalp, would cause deep and painful wounds, which would bleed profusely, like all scalp wounds do.

After placing the crown of thorns on his head, the soldiers began to mock Jesus, saying, "Hail, the King of the Jews." Then they spit on him and beat him with a wooden rod before leading him away to be crucified.

The Crossbar Burden

A man ordered to be crucified was forced to carry his own cross-bar—the horizontal beam of the cross called the *patibulum*—from the prison to the place of his execution. The crossbar weighed nearly one hundred pounds and was strapped to the victim's shoulders with thick rope, which meant that the weight of the wood rested on the lower neck and upper spine—areas savagely wounded from the whipping. If the victim stumbled, his head could be seriously injured. He was unable to protect his face since his hands were tied.

Crucifixion with Nails

When they reached the execution site, the victim was nailed or bound by ropes to the cross. These nails were driven into the bones of the wrist, as the palms could not support the entire body weight. The median nerve runs across the wrist joint and when the nail came in contact with this joint it caused the maximum amount of pain.

And for the feet to be pierced with nails, the legs were twisted into an unnatural and agonizing position.

Many have questioned the historical accuracy of the nailing of the hands and feet because there has been almost zero historical evidence of the practice. Dr. J. W. Hewitt, in his *Harvard Theological Review* article entitled "The Use of Nails in the Crucifixion," said, "To sum up, there is astonishingly little evidence that the feet of a crucified person were ever pierced by nails."[8] He went on to say that the victim's hands and feet were tied to the cross by rope.

For years Dr. Hewitt's statement was considered the final word. The conclusion by many scholars was that the New Testament account of Christ being nailed to the cross was false and misleading. Crucifixion by use of nails was considered legendary. They thought the nails would rip the flesh and be unable to support a body on the cross. Then a major archaeological discovery was made in June 1968. Archaeologist V. Taaferis, under the direction of the Israeli Department of Antiquities and Museums, discovered the remains of a victim, named Yohanan, who had been crucified. The tomb where he was found dates back to the first century A.D. A seven-inch spike had been driven through Yohanan's ankle bone with small pieces of the olive wood cross still attached.

This discovery from the time of Christ adds solid archaeological evidence that crucifixion by nailing was definitely practiced. No longer is the claim based only upon literary evidence.

Breaking the Victim's Legs

The bones of Yohanan confirm another passage in the New Testament: "So the soldiers came and broke the legs of the two men crucified with Jesus. But when they came to Jesus, they saw that he was already dead, so they didn't break his legs" (John 19:32-33). Dr. N. Haas, of the department of anatomy of the Hebrew University and the Haddash Medical School, examined Yohanan's skeletal remains. He concluded that his legs were indeed broken and that "the percussion, passing the already crushed right calf bones, was a harsh and severing blow for the left one, attached as they were to the sharp-edged wooden cross."[9] Two other ancient sources also mention the breaking of legs during crucifixion, confirming the historical nature of the New Testament account.[10]

How Crucifixion Brings About Death

To understand why the victim's legs were broken, we have to understand what crucifixion does to the body. While hanging from the cross, it was very hard for the accused to breathe. To inhale and exhale properly, he had to pull himself up by his hands and feet, which caused searing pain. In time the victim became so exhausted from the effort and from loss of blood that he could no longer perform the breathing motions, and he suffocated.

If the Romans wanted to hasten the victim's death, the usual method of terminating a crucifixion was known as crucifracture. It consisted of the breaking of the leg bones with a club to prevent the victim from pushing upward to breathe. After breaking the legs, death came quickly. Roman soldiers broke the legs of the two thieves crucified with Jesus, but his were not because they saw that he already was dead.

The Spilling of Blood and Water

After Jesus died, one of the executioners rammed a spear into his side, and "immediately blood and water flowed out" (John 19:34). This practice is mentioned in the late first century by Quintillian in *Declamationes maiores* 6:9: "As for those who die on the cross, the executioner does not forbid the burying of those who have been pierced." Many doctors have agreed that the release of blood and water from such a spear wound is a sure sign of death.[11]

British author Michael Green explains the significance of this procedure:

> We are told on eyewitness authority that "blood and water" came out of the pierced side of Jesus (John 19:34-35). The eyewitness clearly attached great importance to this. Had Jesus been alive when the spear pierced His side, strong spouts of blood would have emerged with every heartbeat. Instead, the observer noticed semi-solid dark red clot seeping out, distinct and separate from the accompanying watery serum. This is evidence of massive clotting of the blood in the main arteries, and is exceptionally strong medical proof of death. It is all the more impressive because the evangelist could not possibly have realized its significance to a pathologist. The "blood and water" from the spear-thrust is proof positive that Jesus was already dead.[12]

Pilate required certification of Christ's death before the body could be turned over to Joseph of Arimathea.[13] He consented to Jesus being removed from the cross only after four executioners had certified his death.

Roman Executionary Efficiency

People simply did not survive crucifixion. The methods were too severe and the soldiers too efficient. If there was any hint of survival, the soldiers would continue the process until the victim was dead. Survival was not an option.

There is no doubt that these security precautions taken by the Romans to ensure the death of Jesus were efficient. They worked. Jesus was definitely dead. History does not doubt this fact at all. There is significant evidence for Jesus' death from non-Christian sources. These include Cornelius Tacitus (A.D. 55–120), who is considered by many to be the greatest ancient Roman historian; the Jewish scholar Josephus (A.D. 37–97); and the Jewish Talmud (A.D. 70–200). The death of Jesus is mentioned twelve times in these ancient sources, which date from approximately 20 to 150 years after the death of Jesus. This is remarkable from the perspective of historical analysis.

> **There is no doubt that these security precautions taken by the Romans to ensure the death of Jesus were efficient.**

This is why leading liberal scholars such as John Dominic Crossan believe the execution of Jesus is as certain as any historical fact can be.[14] By trying hard to prevent any kind of fraudulent later claims that the man they were to kill came back to life, Christ's enemies did investigators the great favor of providing powerful evidences of his death that we would not otherwise have. The fact that Jesus was actually killed is as certain as any event recorded in history.

FACT VS. FICTION

Bacchus spat, pushing the saliva into the ground with the toe of his leather boot. He surveyed the courtyard where his men rested, seeking what little warmth they could find on the chill evening.

Two more months and I can leave this God-forsaken outpost. He smiled at the thought, counting down the days until he could return to his wife and child in Rome.

The courtyard was quiet now, where as earlier that day, an angry mob of Jewish leaders and citizens screamed for the life of one Jewish man.

Bacchus shook his head. The customs of these heathen men were most bizarre. And yet Pilate had dealt with the situation with his usual manner of cowardice, somehow sending the man to his death while washing his hands of any responsibility. Bacchus lifted his head and looked over the city. The day's events were odd indeed. Just after lunch dark clouds settled over Jerusalem and then later in the afternoon the entire region was rocked by an earthquake. The city buzzed with tension as conversations were whispered from one home to the next.

Bacchus heard the footsteps padding along the smooth stone outside Pilate's palace, long before he saw the crowd of religious leaders pile into the courtyard.

"Attention!" he called, rousing his men from their break. The other fifteen soldiers in his guard stood to their feet, spears straight and faces set. Caiaphas and the other religious leaders paraded across the courtyard and stood before him, looks of victory and arrogance plastered across their faces.

"We wish to speak to Pilate," Caiaphas announced, his mouth twisted into a sneer.

Before Bacchus could answer, he heard the footfalls of Pilate on the staircase behind him. He turned to see the Roman Prefect striding purposefully down the steps.

"What do you want?" Pilate barked, the anger in his voice undisguised. "Haven't you caused enough trouble for one day?"

Caiaphas stepped forward, chin jutted out. "We want a guard to stand post over the grave of the criminal Jesus."

"Why should I give my soldiers to you? Send one of your temple guards if you're so worried."

The color rose in Caiaphas's face and his voice trembled as he tried to restrain the anger. "Do you not remember what that deceiver once said while he was still alive: 'After three days I will rise from the dead'? So we request that you seal the tomb until the third day. This will prevent his disciples from coming and stealing his body and then telling everyone he was raised from the dead! If that happens, we'll be worse off than we were at first."

Pilate thought about this for a moment. Finally he looked at Bacchus and nodded. "Take your guards and secure the tomb."

Bacchus clenched his jaw but did not speak. Instead he cast a glance at his men. It was their night off.

The Jewish priests turned to leave and motioned after Bacchus and his men to follow as though they were dogs on a leash. He swallowed the curse that rose in his throat, but did as Pilate ordered. He stepped forward and one by one his men fell into ranks behind him.

The march took less than fifteen minutes. Caiaphas led Bacchus and his men to a freshly chiseled rock tomb. Across its opening was a massive slab of rock that had been rolled down a carved groove in front of the cave and set in place by gravity. In order to move the stone, at least four grown men would need to push the stone uphill a minimum of ten feet. Given the difficulty, it was unlikely any man would try.

"Make sure no one even approaches the grave," Caiaphas ordered, and then led the priests away.

"Seal it," Bacchus told his men. "And get comfortable. We're going to be here for three days."

His men, usually feisty, had remained quiet until that moment. "All of this for one dead man?"

Bacchus looked around the quiet countryside. "I don't give the orders. I just follow them."

The muttering continued, not to the point of belligerence, but enough to make Bacchus aware of how disgruntled they were. They should be sleeping on cots in the barracks and instead they found themselves drawing straws for who would take the first watch on this cold night. As luck would have it, Bacchus found himself on duty. While the other twelve men settled in front of the tomb to rest, he and the three remaining guards placed the Roman seal across the tomb with rope. In simple words it declared a penalty of death to anyone who touched the grave without the approval of Pilate. Then they took positions, standing before the grave, spears pointed heavenward and shields drawn across their chests. Those not on duty were spread across the ground on their backs in a semicircle, heads pointing toward the grave. Every four hours, another unit of four was awakened, and those who had been awake took their turn to sleep. They rotated this way around the clock until early Sunday morning.

Bacchus was less than an hour into his shift when he felt the change. All his nerve endings sensed that someone was near. He couldn't hear or see an intruder so much as feel one. The sun had not risen, and the pre-dawn sky was only just beginning to release the slightest hint of silver. Then for the second time in three days, the ground began to rumble. All sixteen soldiers jolted to their feet, looking at one another in fright. And the last thing that Bacchus would be able to recall about the event for the rest of his life was that a blinding white light in the form of a man flooded his vision. He felt the fear rising in his blood like a tidal wave, unlike anything he'd ever known in battle or life. And then all was darkness as he fell to the ground in a dead faint.

When Bacchus woke a short time later, he knew that his life was forfeit, and that he would never see his wife or child again. Not only had the seal been broken, but the stone was gone—not just rolled away from the entrance—but literally picked up and thrown twenty feet away. He did not need to enter the tomb to know that it was empty. He did not need to recite the soldier's creed to know that he and his men had failed in their jobs. He did not need to wonder what Pilate would say or do. He knew all these things. He knew that before the day was out, he and his men would draw straws to take the blame for what happened, and one of them, most likely Bacchus himself, would burn alive in his own garments.

"Get up!" he shouted, rousing his men from sleep as an idea occurred to him. "If you care for your life you will come with me and do as I say."

"Captain," one of his men asked. "Where are we going?"

A grimace spread across his face. It was distasteful but it was the only choice they had. "To the Chief Priest. He is the only one who has power over Pilate."

"What will we tell him?"

Bacchus picked up his spear and slung his shield over his shoulder. "We'll tell him the truth and he can sort out the details."

"Caiaphas won't like hearing the truth."

Bacchus nodded. "He never does."

Resurrection Facts to Be Reckoned With

If you want to explain away the events surrounding the resurrection, you must deal with certain facts. Both the Jews and Romans outwitted themselves when they took such pains to make sure Jesus died and remained in the grave. The reality that something happened in spite of their security precautions—crucifixion, burial, entombment, sealing, and guarding the tomb—makes it very difficult to defend a position that Christ has not been raised from the dead. Let's consider these historical facts for a moment:

Fact Number 1: The Roman Seal Was Broken

On Easter morning the seal that stood for the power and authority of the Roman Empire was broken. No one denies this fact.

Matthew records that "along with the guard they set a seal on the stone" (Matthew 27:66, *NASB*). The stone could be sealed only in the presence of the Roman guards who were left in charge. The purpose of this procedure was to prevent anyone from tampering with the grave's contents.

After the guard inspected the tomb and rolled the stone in place, a cord was stretched across the rock and fastened at either end with sealing clay. Finally, the clay packs were stamped with the official signet of the Roman governor.

> **Because the seal on Christ's tomb was Roman, it verified the fact that Jesus' body was protected from vandals by nothing less than the power of the Roman Empire.**

Henry Sumner Maine, former member of the Supreme Council of India, and former professor of civil law at the University of Cambridge, said of the Roman seal, "Seals in antiquity were actually considered as a mode of authentication."[1] To authenticate something simply means to prove that it is real or genuine. Because the seal was Roman, it also verified the fact that Christ's body was protected from vandals by nothing less than the power and authority of the Roman Empire. Anyone trying to move the stone would have broken the seal and thus incurred the wrath of Roman law and power.

A death sentence was required punishment for anyone who broke that seal. The Roman equivalent of the FBI was immediately called into action to find the person responsible. Would Christ's disciples have broken that seal? Hardly! After his arrest they showed signs of craven cowardice and hid themselves. Peter even denied that he knew Christ.

Fact Number 2: The Tomb Was Empty

Another undeniable fact that Sunday morning was the empty tomb. No one has ever denied that the tomb was empty. After the resurrection, Jesus' disciples did not go off to Athens or Rome to preach that he had been resurrected; they went right back to the city of Jerusalem where their message would have been easily disproved if they lied. The tomb was a fifteen minute walk from the center of Jerusalem. The resurrection claim could not have been maintained for a moment in Jerusalem if the tomb had not been empty.

Both Jewish and Roman history acknowledges an empty tomb. These sources range from the Jewish historian Josephus to a compilation of fifth-century Jewish writings called the *Toledoth Jeshu*. Maier calls this "positive evidence from a hostile source, which is the strongest kind of historical evidence. In essence, this means that if a source admits a fact decidedly *not* in its favor, then that fact is genuine."[2]

Considering that both Christians and Jews agreed that the body of Jesus was not in the tomb, the best historical explanation is that the tomb was really empty.

Even today it is common for the burial place of a significant religious leader to become a shrine. Muslims take yearly pilgrimages to Mecca in honor of Mohammed. Hindus and Buddhists visit the graves of their spiritual guides, and Jews visit the grave of Abraham in Hebron. Why didn't Jesus' tomb become a shrine? The best explanation seems to be that the tomb was really empty, and thus there would be no good reason to worship it as a shrine. When Christians go to see Christ's burial spot, they visit an empty tomb. What other religious group does this?

One of the most compelling pieces of evidence showing that the tomb was empty is the fact that it was first discovered by women. In first century Palestine, women had a low status as citizens or legal witnesses. Except in rare circumstances, Jewish law precluded women from giving testimony in a court of law. Why would those who wanted to advance Christianity have created a legend that embarrassed the disciples by having *them* flee during the crucifixion and yet have *women* discover the empty tomb? Common sense tells us that the only reason women were reported as the first witnesses is because it was the truth.

If the resurrection story was simply fabricated, women would never have been included as the first witnesses to the empty tomb.

Even the highly respected and accomplished historian Michael Grant, himself not a follower of Christ, concludes, "But if we apply the same sort of criteria that we would apply to any other ancient literary sources, then the evidence is firm and plausible enough to necessitate the conclusion that the tomb was indeed found empty."[3]

Fact Number 3: The Large Stone Was Moved

The first thing that impressed the people who approached the tomb that Sunday morning was the unusual position of the two-ton stone that had previously been lodged in front of the doorway. All of the gospel writers mention the removal of this enormous stone.

In fact, the stone was in such a position up a slope away from the entire massive sepulcher that John (in chapter 20 of his Gospel) had to use a different Greek verb, *airo*, which means "to pick something up and carry it away."

If the disciples had come and tiptoed around the sleeping guards, why would they have moved the two-ton stone up a slope away from the entire massive grave to such a position that it looked like someone had picked it up and carried it away? The needless effort would have been noisy and taken valuable time and energy. Those soldiers would have been deaf not to have heard the commotion.

Fact Number 4: The Roman Guard Went AWOL
The Roman guard fled when the stone was moved. This is a very odd fact to consider. Dr. George Currie, who carefully studied the military discipline of the Romans, reports that the death penalty was required for various duty failures such as desertion, losing or disposing of one's weapons, betraying plans to an enemy, refusing to protect an officer, and leaving the night watch. To that list, one can add "falling asleep."

One form of execution was to strip the guard of his clothes, then burn him alive in a fire started with the garments. The history of Roman discipline and security testifies to the fact that if the tomb had not been empty the soldiers never would have left their position. Fear of the wrath of their superiors and the ensuing death penalty meant they paid close attention to the most minute details of their job.

Dr. Bill White, formerly in charge of the Garden Tomb in Jerusalem, has extensively studied the resurrection and subsequent events following the first Easter. White makes several critical observations about the Jewish authorities bribing the Roman guard:

> If the stone were simply rolled to one side of the tomb, as would be necessary to enter it, then they might be justified in accusing the men of sleeping at their posts, and in punishing them severely. If the men protested that the earthquake broke the seal and that the stone rolled

CONSIDER THIS

Even though there was no body present
on that Sunday morning, the tomb did
contain an amazing phenomenon. When John
arrived at the tomb, he looked over to the
place where the body of Jesus had lain.
There were graveclothes, in the form
of the body, slightly caved in and empty—
like the empty chrysalis of a caterpillar's
cocoon. John never did get over it.
The first thing that stuck in the minds of
the disciples was the empty graveclothes—
undisturbed in their form and position.
A grave robber would not have been
able to remove the body without
destroying the graveclothes.

back under vibration, they would still be liable to punishment for behavior which might be labeled cowardice.

But these possibilities do not meet the case. There was some undeniable evidence which made it impossible for the chief priests to bring any charge against the guard. The Jewish authorities must have visited the scene, examined the stone, and recognized its position as making it humanly impossible for their men to have permitted its removal. No twist of human ingenuity could provide an adequate answer or a scapegoat and so they were forced to bribe the guard and seek to hush things.[4]

Fact Number 5: The Graveclothes Tell a Tale

Even though there was no body present on that Sunday morning, the tomb did hold something. It contained an amazing phenomenon. After visiting the tomb and seeing the stone rolled away, the women ran back and told the disciples. Then Peter and John took off running. John outran Peter and, upon arriving at the tomb, he did not enter. He looked over to the place where the body of Jesus had lain. There were graveclothes, *in the form of the body, slightly caved in and empty*—like the empty chrysalis of a caterpillar's cocoon. He never did get over it.

The first thing that stuck in the minds of the disciples was the empty graveclothes—undisturbed in their form and position. A grave robber would not have been able to remove the body without destroying the graveclothes.

Fact Number 6: Christ's Confirmed Appearances

Few scholars today doubt that the disciples at least believed they saw the risen Jesus. Reginald Fuller has boldly claimed that "within a few weeks after the crucifixion Jesus' disciples came to believe this is one of the indisputable facts of history."[5] What caused the disciples to have this belief? From day one the church has claimed that Jesus personally appeared to his followers.

Peter sat in the boat, his body accustomed to a lifetime of gentle rocking on open water. The Sea of Galilee was calm that night and yet their nets remained empty. The small fishing vessel was full of men nodding off to sleep in the hours before dawn. They worked all the previous evening and into the night, doing their best to bring in a load of fish that they could sell at market that day. Yet time and again, the nets were hauled in dripping wet but totally empty.

So Peter sat in the darkness as his friends dozed, unable to chase the thoughts from his mind.

"Jesus is alive," he murmured into the silence. It was an amazing statement that even now threatened to take his breath away. And yet he sat in this boat, having returned to his former life. For three years he had followed Jesus around Israel, believing every word he said, but for some reason he did not know what to do with those words now that Christ was risen. He was suspended between two lives, the former and the new.

These things rolled around his mind as the sun slipped over the horizon and flooded the lake with golden light. One by one his friends woke and began to rub their eyes. The boat drifted near the shore, nets still empty.

Thomas was the first to see a man standing on the beach. He held a hand over his eyes, shielding them from the light.

"Good morning! Did you catch anything for breakfast?" the stranger called from the shore.

"No," Thomas shouted as he fiddled with the nets.

"Throw the net off the right side of the boat and see what happens," he suggested.

Thomas and Peter exchanged a humorous look. As though switching sides of the boat would make any difference. But they humored him anyway and dragged the nets across the boat and slid them into the water on the other side.

"Peter," Thomas said, shaking his shoulder. "Peter, look!"

Suddenly the boat began to tip to the left as the net filled with fish. Within moments the net was so burdened with fish they weren't strong enough to pull it aboard.

All the while John stood at the back of the boat, his eyes on the distant figure that stood on the shore. "Peter," he said, his eyes drawn wide. He pointed at the stranger. "It's Jesus."

A great cry of excitement went up from those in the fishing vessel and they scrambled for the oars. Peter on the other hand stood frozen where he was, his gaze fixed on Jesus. Even though he was tempted to help them get to shore, he remembered that night in Caiaphas's courtyard when he had denied Jesus three times. And worst of all, he remembered the look on Jesus' face as they led him away, the look of betrayal.

Then Peter panicked. Instead of grabbing an oar, he dove headfirst into the sea. In their excitement to get to shore, his friends did not notice. Within moments they were dragging the boat across the rocks and running to greet Jesus. Peter on the other hand remained where he was, treading water. He knew there was no running from Jesus. And yet he did not know how to look him in the face at that moment. Yet there was no option other than to swim to shore and hear whatever Jesus would say. He must take the rebuke that was due him.

A small fire crackled on the shore and several fish roasted over the orange flames. A basket of warm bread sat beside the fire.

As Peter pulled himself from the water, he grabbed the net and pulled it ashore, straining beneath its weight and looking for any excuse not to approach the fire.

"Bring some of the fish you've just caught," Jesus said, inviting him closer.

Peter could not deny him. He brought a handful of fish and settled beside the fire, letting its warmth soak into his wet clothing. Try as he might, Peter could not look at Jesus, could not meet his eyes for fear of what he might find there.

Jesus took the bread and gave it to them. He did the same with the fish. This was now the third time Jesus had shown himself alive to them and they still did not know what to make of him.

After breakfast Peter could feel Jesus' eyes on him, could feel the heat as they bore into his heart.

His words were gentle and the kindness was agonizing to Peter as he heard the words, "Peter, son of John, do you love me?"

His will broke and he finally looked into the eyes of his risen Lord. The words bunched in his throat and he could barely choke them out, "Yes, Master, you know I love you."

Twice more Jesus asked this question, and each time Peter's heart broke. Finally in desperation he cried, "Master, you know everything there is to know. You've got to know that I love you!"

Jesus smiled and his gaze spoke right to Peter's heart. And in that moment he knew what Christ wanted of him: his life. Every bit of it. This Jesus, his risen Lord, wanted Peter to live in such a way that every person he met would come to know the same love and forgiveness that Jesus bestowed on him. It no longer mattered that Peter had walked away from him that night in the courtyard. What mattered was that Jesus was here in this moment and he wanted Peter to follow him, even if it meant to the death.

The Large Number of Eyewitnesses

When studying an event in history, it is important to investigate whether the eyewitnesses were alive when the event happened. Greater numbers of witnesses help to validate the accuracy of the published report. For instance, if we all witness a murder, and in a week the police report turns out to be composed of fabricated lies, we as eyewitnesses can refute the report. When a book is written about an event, the accuracy of its content can be validated if enough eyewitnesses or participants in the event are alive when the book is published.

One of the earliest records of Christ's appearing after the resurrection is by Paul in 1 Corinthians 15:3-8:

I passed on to you what was most important and what had also been passed on to me. Christ died for our sins just as the Scriptures said. He was buried, and he was raised from the dead on the third day, just as the Scriptures said. He was seen by Peter and then by the Twelve. After that, he was seen by more than 500 of his followers at one time, most of whom are still alive, though some have died. Then he was seen by James and later by all the apostles. Last of all, as though I had been born at the wrong time, I also saw him.

Virtually all scholars agree that in these verses Paul records an ancient creed, or tradition, that dates before the writing of 1 Corinthians (mid-50s A.D.). In fact, most scholars who have investigated this creed date it to within three to eight years after Christ's crucifixion.[6]

In these verses, Paul appeals to his audience's knowledge of the fact that Christ had been seen by more than five hundred people at one time. Paul reminds them that the majority of these people were still alive and could be questioned. This statement is as strong evidence as anyone could hope to find for something that happened two thousand years ago.

This is why Dr. Norman Geisler has concluded that the appearance to the five hundred "has the ring of truth about it,"[7] and William Lane Craig claims that "it is nearly indisputable that this appearance took place."[8] Paul never could have claimed that Jesus appeared to five hundred witnesses so soon after the event if the event had not actually occurred.

If each of these five hundred people were to testify in a courtroom for only six minutes each, including all of the cross-examinations, you would have an amazing fifty hours of first-hand eyewitness testimony. Add to this the testimony of the many other eyewitnesses and you could well have the largest trial in history.

The Variety of Witnesses and Locations

Another factor often overlooked in determining the credibility of the witnesses is the variety of people who saw the risen Jesus and the variety of locations in which they saw him. Professor Merrill C. Tenney writes:

> It is noteworthy that these appearances are not stereotyped. No two of them are exactly alike. The appearance to Mary Magdalene occurred in early morning; that to the travelers to Emmaus in the afternoon; and to the apostles in the evening, probably after dark. He appeared to Mary in the open air. Mary was alone when she saw Him; the disciples were together in a group; and Paul records that on one occasion He appeared to more than 500 at one time.
>
> The reactions also were varied. Mary was overwhelmed with emotion; the disciples were frightened; Thomas was obstinately incredulous when told of the Lord's resurrection, but worshipped Him when He manifested Himself. Each occasion had its own peculiar atmosphere and characteristics, and revealed some different quality of the risen Lord.[9]

In no way can one say his appearances were made up. Each was unique to the individual and the situation.

The Inclusion of Hostile Witnesses

A third factor crucial to proving Christ's resurrection is that he appeared to those who were hostile to him. In an attempt to dilute the overwhelming impact of the eyewitness accounts, skeptics often claim that his post-resurrection appearances were all to friends and followers. Despite the popularity of this claim, it is false.

No reasonable person would consider Saul of Tarsus to have been a follower of Christ. He despised Christ and persecuted Christians, aiming to eradicate the entire Christian movement. Yet Saul, whose name was later changed to Paul, became one of the greatest propagators of the Christian movement in history. What could account for this radical transformation? Nothing short of a personal appearance by the risen Jesus could have sufficed.

> ## What could account for Paul's radical transformation? Nothing short of a personal appearance by the risen Jesus could have sufficed.

Consider James, the brother of Jesus. The Gospel record indicates that none of Jesus' brothers believed in him during his lifetime (see John 7:5; Mark 3:21-35). In fact, they tried to fool Jesus into a death trap at a public feast in Jerusalem. Yet James later became a follower of his brother and joined the band of persecuted Christians, becoming a key leader in the church and one of its early martyrs, as attested by Josephus, Hegesippus, and Clement of Alexandria.[10] What caused such a change in his attitude? The best historical explanation is that the risen Jesus appeared also to James.

In spite of the elaborate precautions the Jews and Romans took to keep his body in the tomb, several facts attest to the conclusion that he returned to life and left the tomb.

Tom Anderson, former president of the California Trial Lawyers Association and co-author of the Basic Advocacy Manual of the Association of Trial Lawyers of America, says, "Let's assume that Christ did not rise from the dead. Let's assume that the written accounts of His appearances to hundreds of people are false. I want to pose a question. With an event so well publicized, don't you think that it's reasonable that one historian, one eyewitness, one antagonist would record for all time that he had seen Christ's body: 'Listen, I saw that tomb—it was not empty! Look, I was there, Christ did not rise from the dead. As a matter of fact, I saw Christ's body.' The silence of history is deafening when it comes to testimony against the resurrection."[11]

In the thirty years since Jesus walked the dusty roads of Palestine Dr. Luke had seen many things. The world itself had been turned on its head. He sat before the window on that summer night, the breeze rustling the pages before him and he thought about what he wanted his young friend Theophilus to know about a Jesus he never met.

The better half of Luke's life had been spent telling others about those events, about the stories that Jesus told while breaking bread, about the day they hauled him from the garden and took him to a mock trial, about watching his life drain away on a Roman cross, and about the day that his Lord rose into the air and left them all behind to finish the story. He had been faithful in telling all those things. And yet he knew the number of his days was slowly fading. There would come a day that this eyewitness was no longer on this earth.

It was for such a reason that Luke grabbed the parchment and quill and spread them before him on the table. If he had just one chance to write this story for his young friend, what would he say?

Luke closed his old, watery eyes for a moment, as he asked for wisdom, and then he grabbed the quill with wrinkled bony fingers. He dipped the feather in the ink well, tapped it twice against the side of the jar, and began to write. His hand swept across the parchment, steadier than one would think for a man of his age. As he scribbled the words, he nodded in agreement, the memories coming fresh.

"Yes," he muttered. "Yes. This is what I need to be doing."

And so it was on that night that the doctor called Luke, a man who mended bodies for the better part of his life, wrote words that would mend souls for all of human history . . .

So many others have tried their hand at putting together a story of the wonderful harvest of Scripture and history that took place among us, using reports handed down by the original eyewitnesses who served this Word with their very lives. Since I have investigated all the reports in close detail, starting from the story's beginning, I decided to write it all out for you, most honorable Theophilus, so you can know beyond the shadow of a doubt the reliability of what you were taught . . .

The New Testament provides the primary historical source for information on the resurrection. Because it makes claims about divine intervention in human affairs, many critics during the nineteenth, twentieth and twenty-first centuries have attacked the reliability of the New Testament as a historical document. Do these critics have a basis for their attack other than their doubt that the miraculous can occur?

The original manuscripts that Matthew, Mark, Luke, John, Paul and Peter actually wrote have long since decayed or been lost. The New Testament is based on copies of these original manuscripts—not only copies, but copies of copies through a period of almost two thousand years. So how can we know if what we read today is what the disciples actually wrote so long ago? To determine whether the New Testament is a legitimate historical document, we have to know two things: how close was it written to the death, burial, and resurrection of Christ, and how many copies of the original documents are in existence today?

What Is the Time Span Between the Death of Christ and the Writing of the New Testament?

For years, critics have assumed that the New Testament Scriptures were a couple hundred years after Jesus died. They believed that these writings came basically from myths or legends that developed during the lengthy interval between the lifetime of Jesus and the time they were actually written. By the end of the nineteenth century, however, archaeological finds confirmed the accuracy of the New Testament manuscripts. Discoveries of early *papyri* manuscripts bridged the gap between the time of Christ and existing manuscripts from a later date.[12] These findings greatly increased the confidence of scholars in the reliability of the Bible. They concluded that the New Testament is the work of the apostles themselves, or of contemporaries who worked with them.

Craig Blomberg says, "All of this adds up to a strong case that all three [Synoptic] Gospels [Matthew, Mark and Luke] were composed within about thirty years of Christ's death (probably A.D. 30) and well within the period of time when people could check up on the accuracy of the facts they contain."[13] While the Gospel of John is typically placed in the 90s, this is still far closer to the events than the manuscripts of many ancient biographies that historians accept without question. For example, the two earliest biographers of Alexander the Great, Plutarch and Arian, wrote more than four hundred years after Alexander's death in 323 B.C., yet their writings are generally accepted as trustworthy by historians.[14]

How Many Copies of the Original Documents Are in Existence Today?

Regarding the date between original writing and existing copies, most ancient works have a gap of more than 700 years, with some works, such as Plato and Aristotle, being twice that. In contrast, there are fragments of the Gospel of John dating within 40 to 50 years of the original writing (*John Rylands Papyri*) and a nearly complete copy of the New Testament within 100 to 150 years of its writing (*Chester Beatty Papyri*). Historically speaking, existing copies of the New Testament books are astonishingly close to the originals.

When I [Josh] finished my research into biblical reliability and released the first *Evidence That Demands a Verdict* in 1973, I was able to document 14,000 manuscripts of the New Testament alone. Now, after the release of *The New Evidence That Demands a Verdict*, I am able to document nearly 25,000 manuscripts. This number of copies makes the New Testament far and away the best documented writing in ancient history. Its nearest competitor is Homer's *Iliad* with 643 manuscript copies existing. Some recent critics, such as Bart Ehrman (*Misquoting Jesus*), have claimed that there are too many contradictions in these manuscripts to reconstruct the original with confidence. But this conclusion is far too hasty. For one thing, 80 percent of the variations are spelling errors. While there are a handful of minor texts upon which New Testament scholars disagree, *there is no textual variation that threatens a central Christian doctrine.*

The number of manuscripts and their closeness to the original documents authenticating the New Testament motivated Sir Frederick Kenyon, regarded as one of the greatest archaeologists ever, to write:

> The interval, then, between the dates of original composition and the earliest extant evidence becomes so small as to be in fact negligible, and the last foundation for any doubt that the Scriptures have come down to us substantially as they were written now has been removed. Both the authenticity and the general integrity of the books of the New Testament may be regarded as finally established.[15]

CONSIDER THIS

There are nearly 25,000 manuscripts
of the New Testament that can be
documented, which makes the New
Testament far and away the best
documented writing in ancient history.
Some recent critics have claimed that
there are too many contradictions in these
manuscripts to reconstruct the original
with confidence. But this conclusion is
far too hasty. For one thing, 80 percent
of the variations are spelling errors.
While there are a handful of minor texts upon
which New Testament scholars disagree,
there is no textual variation that
threatens a central Christian doctrine.

John A. T. Robinson concluded, "The wealth of manuscripts, and above all the narrow interval of time between the writing and the earliest extant copies, make it by far the best attested text of any ancient writing in the world."[16]

Another reason for trusting the New Testament record of Christ is that it was written by eyewitnesses or from eyewitness accounts.

- 2 Peter 1:16 says, "For we did not follow cleverly devised tales when we made known to you the power and coming of our Lord Jesus Christ, but we were *eyewitnesses* of His majesty" (*NASB*).

- 1 John 1:1: "We proclaim to you the one who existed from the beginning, whom we have heard and seen. We saw him with our own eyes and touched him with our own hands. He is the Word of life."

- The disciples said, "He also presented Himself alive after His suffering, by many convincing proofs, appearing to them over a period of forty days" (Acts 1:3, *NASB*).

- Acts 2:32: "This Jesus God raised up again, to which we are all *witnesses*" (*NASB*).

- John says, "And he who has seen has testified, and his testimony is true; and he knows that he is telling the truth, so that you also may believe" (19:35, *NASB*).

- "This disciple is the one who testifies to these events and has recorded them here. And we know that his account of these things is accurate" (John 21:24).

In recording the events of the resurrection, the disciples followed the Jewish law, which required an honest witness. John Ankerburg and John Weldon put it this way: "The fact that the apostles constantly appealed to such eyewitness testimony is all the more believable in light of their own unique Jewish heritage. No religion has ever stressed the importance of truth or truthful testimony more than the Jewish religion."[17] In the Jewish Scriptures, God constantly warned his people to tell the truth. In fact, the disciples knew that if they gave false testimony they would be considered false witnesses against God and could be punished by death (see Exodus 20:16; 23:1; Deuteronomy 17:6; 19:15; Proverbs 19:5,9).

In further support of their testimony, the apostles refused to renounce their beliefs regarding the resurrected Christ even though they faced harsh persecution and martyrdom for believing. The disciples went to the grave with the conviction that they had seen the risen Jesus. It is only fair to trust their testimony.

Further corroboration for the New Testament documents comes from archaeology. Where the Gospels can be tested, archaeological discoveries have constantly proven the documents to be accurate. Here are just a few examples of how archaeology has confirmed the biblical record:

- For centuries there had been no record of the court where Pilate tried Jesus. William Albright shows that this court was the court of the Tower of Antonia, the Roman military headquarters in Jerusalem.[18]

- The pool of Bethesda, as mentioned in John 5:2, has been identified, "with a fair measure of certainty in the northeast quarter of the old city (the areas called Bezetha, or

'New Lawn') in the first century A.D., where traces of its earlier existence were discovered in the course of excavations near the Church of St. Anne in 1888."[19]

• In 1990 the burial ground of Caiaphas, the Jewish high priest who sent Jesus to Pilate, and his family was found in Jerusalem.[20]

Extra-Biblical Evidence

Sources outside the Bible provide a great deal of support for the Jesus recorded in the New Testament. While these sources do not provide the detail of the Gospels, they do provide powerful corroborative evidence for the portrait of Jesus as portrayed in the Gospels.

Historical Jesus expert Gary Habermas has argued that "ancient extra-biblical sources do present a surprisingly large amount of detail concerning both the life of Jesus and the nature of early Christianity."[21] He notes that, "Overall, at least seventeen non-Christian writings record more than fifty details concerning the life, teachings, death, and resurrection of Jesus, plus details concerning the earliest church."[22] Edwin Yamauchi, professor of history at Miami University, lists what we know about Jesus through non-Christian writers alone:

Jesus was a Jewish teacher; (2) many people believed that he performed healings and exorcisms; (3) he was rejected by the Jewish leaders; (4) he was crucified under Pontius Pilate in the reign of Tiberius; (5) despite this shameful death, his followers, who believed that he was still alive, spread beyond Palestine so that there were multitudes of them in Rome by A.D. 64; (6) all kinds of people from the cities and countryside—men and women, slave and free—worshiped him as God by the beginning of the second century.[23]

While the majority of the details concerning the life of Jesus in the New Testament are found in the Gospels, Paul's writings contain significant information that affirm and corroborate those events. Professor Gary Habermas explains the significance of Paul's letters regarding the historical Jesus:

> Paul provides the most details concerning the last week of Jesus' life, speaking frequently of these events due to their centrality to the gospel. He gives particulars concerning the Lord's Supper, even citing the words Jesus spoke on this occasion (1 Corinthians 11:23-25). Paul speaks often of Jesus' death (Romans 4:25; 5:8), specifying crucifixion (Romans 6:6; Galatians 2:20) and mentioning the Jewish instigation of it (1 Thessalonians 2:14-15). He tells how Jesus was buried, rose again three days later, and appeared to numerous people, both individually and in groups (1 Corinthians 15:3-8).[24]

Based on the historical facts, it is no wonder so many scholars have concluded that the New Testament is the best documented of all the ancient writings. In terms of the number and variety of documents and the time period between the events and the writings, none other matches it in its integrity.[25]

Throughout history there have been many spiritual leaders, messiahs, gurus and prophets who claim to answer our deepest questions—Muhammad, Plato, Buddha, Gandhi, Krishna, Joseph Smith, and so on. At first appearance, Jesus seems to be in the same category as these people, another religious leader peddling answers to life's baffling questions.

There are many claims that various gods exist, but only one God cared enough to become a man and die on our behalf. Of the ninety-nine names for Allah in Islam, not one of them is either Father or Love. Buddha did not come and personally indwell his disciples. No other religion besides Christianity tells of a God who loves his people so much that he would endure the hellish pain of the cross in order for us to know him personally.

> **There are many claims that various gods exist, but only one God cared enough to become a man and die on our behalf.**

The resurrection is the key to every promise of the Christian faith. The claim of eternal life with a loving God is meaningless unless the resurrection actually occurred. Yet if Christ really died and rose from the grave, as the evidence clearly proves, we can do the same thing. The resurrection was a real event that actually happened at a given time and in a specific place in world history. Jesus lived. He died. And he rose again on the third day. These are facts on which you can hang your faith.

Sean McDowell—Author and speaker

FAQ Info Photos +

◀ **Page 1 of 2** ▶

Frequently Asked Questions About the Resurrection

All Posts Posts by Sean Posts by Others

Sean McDowell is an author, speaker and the head of the Bible department at Capistrano Valley Christian Schools, where he teaches courses on Apologetics, Theology and Old Testament. He is a popular speaker at camps, churches, schools and conferences nationwide. Sean and his wife, Stephanie, have been married for 8 years and have two children, Scottie and Shauna.

See Also:

FAQ—*Evidence for the Resurrection*

FAQ—*Jesus Is Alive*

Jacob writes: A friend told me that Jesus wasn't really dead. He said he was just in a coma, and that his resurrection wasn't really a resurrection as much as just him coming out of a coma. How can I respond to that argument?

Sean says: Some people believe that Jesus didn't really die on the cross. But we have to consider all that happened to Jesus:

(1) He went through six trial cross-examinations—three Roman and three Jewish

(2) He was beaten to bloody shreds by a Roman whip

(3) He was so weak he couldn't carry his own cross to the crucifixion site

(4) He had a crown of thorns shoved into his scalp

(5) He had spikes driven through his hands and feet and hung bleeding for six hours

(6) The Romans thrust a spear deep into his side

(7) He was wrapped in linen and one hundred pounds of spices

(8) A large stone sat against his tomb's entrance

(9) At least sixteen Roman guards were posted outside the tomb; and

(10) A seal was placed across the entrance.

Jacob: Ouch! How could Jesus possibly have survived all of that?

Sean: Good question. According to the coma theory, the damp air inside of the tomb somehow revived him. Then he split out of his garments, singlehandedly pushed the

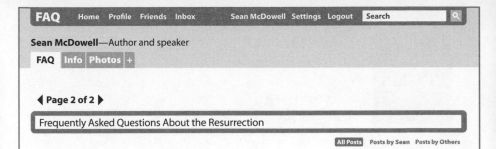

◀ Page 2 of 2 ▶

Frequently Asked Questions About the Resurrection

All Posts   Posts by Sean   Posts by Others

stone away, fought off the guards, walked naked and barefoot on badly wounded feet through a city stirring in the morning, and appeared to his disciples as the Lord of life.

Jacob: LOL! Seems a bit far-fetched.

Sean: I agree. The most significant problem for this particular theory is that it underestimates the severity of Jesus' wounds and all the evidence for his death. Here is why we believe that Jesus really did die during his crucifixion:

(1) His injuries were so severe.

(2) The brutality of crucifixion virtually guarantees death.

(3) The piercing of Jesus' side is medical proof that he had already died.

(4) Jesus said he was in the act of dying while on the cross.

(5) Even though it was customary for soldiers to break the legs of the victims to speed up death, they did not even have to break his because their examination determined that he was already dead.

(6) Pilate summoned the centurion to make sure Jesus had actually died before giving the body to Joseph for burial.

(7) If Jesus had not died from his previous torture, he would have died in the tomb from lack of food, water, and medical treatment while buried under one hundred pounds of spices for three days.

(8) Medical experts and historians who have studied the circumstances surrounding the end of Jesus' life have concluded that he actually died on the cross.

Josh McDowell—Author and speaker

Frequently Asked Questions About the Resurrection

Information

Josh McDowell is a speaker, author and founder of The Josh McDowell Ministry, an organization that reaches young people worldwide with the truth and love of Jesus Christ. He has written or co-written 112 books, which have sold more than 51 million copies worldwide. Josh and his wife, Dottie, have been married 37 years and have four children and two grandchildren.

See Also:

FAQ—*Evidence for the Resurrection*

FAQ—*Jesus Is Alive*

Anna writes: I have read that the Roman guards sealed Jesus' tomb. Why would they bother to do that when they were standing right there?

Josh says: The Gospel of Matthew records that "along with the guard they set a seal on the stone." The stone could be sealed only in the presence of the Roman guards who were left in charge. After the guard inspected the tomb and rolled the stone in place, a cord was stretched across the rock and fastened at either end with sealing clay. Finally, the clay packs were stamped with the official signet of the Roman governor. The reason they did this was to prevent anyone from tampering with Jesus' body. Anyone trying to move the stone would have broken the seal and thus incurred the wrath of Roman law and power.

Sam writes: I know that Christians believe that Jesus was raised from the dead, but aren't there other ways to explain the events surrounding the resurrection?

Josh says: Many theories have been proposed attempting to show that the resurrection of Jesus Christ was a fraud. Since most of the facts surrounding the resurrection are undeniable, these attempts have involved putting a different spin on the facts. Few skeptics deny the essential events—the trial, the crucifixion, the burial, the guards, the seal, or the empty tomb—because the historical evidence supporting these events is too strong.

Sam: I just don't know that those events mean that a dead man came to life again. I think there must be some other explanation.

Josh: It takes more faith to believe some of those theories than to just accept the explanation offered in the New Testament.

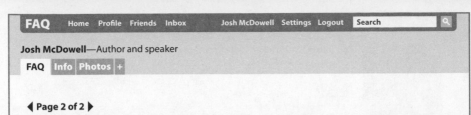

Frequently Asked Questions About the Resurrection

All Posts Posts by Josh Posts by Others

Sam: So what are some of these theories?

Josh: Well, here's a few that are commonly tossed around by skeptics:

- The entire story of Jesus' death and resurrection is a myth.

- No one knows where Jesus was buried, so we can't really know if the tomb was empty.

- The women who discovered the empty tomb actually went to the wrong one, so there is no relevance to the fact that it was found without a body.

- All accounts of the resurrection are legends created hundreds of years after his death.

- Jesus' resurrection was not physical but spiritual.

- The witnesses to Jesus' resurrection were actually hallucinating and did not really see him.

- Jesus wasn't really crucified because God allowed a bystander to take his place.

But when held up against all of the facts and historical evidence, none of these theories can be proven or even seriously considered, whereas the biblical account stands up to the test of historical evidence and proven fact.

Sean McDowell—Author and speaker

FAQ Info Photos +

◀ Page 1 of 2 ▶

Frequently Asked Questions About the Resurrection

Sean McDowell is an author, speaker and the head of the Bible department at Capistrano Valley Christian Schools, where he teaches courses on Apologetics, Theology and Old Testament. He is a popular speaker at camps, churches, schools and conferences nationwide. Sean and his wife, Stephanie, have been married for 8 years and have two children, Scottie and Shauna.

See Also:

FAQ—*Evidence for the Resurrection*

FAQ—*Jesus Is Alive*

All Posts   Posts by Sean   Posts by Others

Heather writes: Since Jesus' resurrection is technically a miracle, doesn't that rule out the possibility that it can be true—since miracles can't be proven by science?

Sean says: Because the resurrection of Jesus was miraculous, our first task is to define a miracle. Dr. Richard Purtill defines a miracle as "an event in which God temporarily makes an exception to the natural order of things, to show that God is acting."[1] Miracles are impossible only if we assume that God does not exist.

Heather: Yes, but we can't prove scientifically that God does exist.

Sean: In this day and age, it is not uncommon for people to believe that nothing can be confirmed as true unless it can be proven scientifically. Students constantly ask me, "Can you prove the resurrection scientifically?" Yet science is applicable only to repeatable events or facts. It is unfortunate that the modern awe of science has led people to mistakenly assume that the scientific method can be used to determine all truth. It cannot, and it never could. It does not even apply to all scientific fields, such as geology or evolutionary biology.

Heather: Then how can we know that any historical event is true?

Sean: Historical events, by their very nature, occur only once in time and are not repeatable. We cannot prove scientifically that Hannibal crossed the Alps because we cannot rouse him from the grave, set up his army, train his elephants again, and repeat the event. But this gives us no reason to look at the historical evidence as a "weak" science. Most reasonable people have confidence in the facts of history because we have other valid methods of determining their truth. As a unique event in history, the

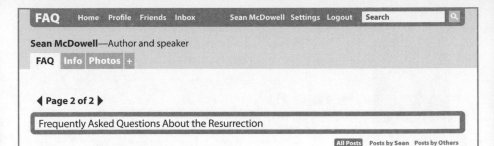
Frequently Asked Questions About the Resurrection

All Posts Posts by Sean Posts by Others

resurrection of Jesus Christ is outside the realm of the scientific method. No wonder so many scholars have concluded that the New Testament is the best documented of all the ancient writings. In terms of the number and variety of documents and the time period between the events and the writings, none other matches it in its integrity.

Caleb writes: Haven't many other people been resurrected? And if so, why is Jesus' resurrection so important?

Sean says: Yes, there are many stories in the Scriptures of people who have died and been raised back to life (see John 11; Acts 9:36-42; 20:7-12, Kings 4:32-35, and Mark 5:40-42). There are even stories of people being raised from the dead in other religions.

Caleb: So what's the big deal about Jesus coming back to life?

Sean: Well, there are two primary differences between these resurrections and that of Jesus. First, all of the people in history who have been raised from the dead, besides Jesus, eventually died again. Two thousand years ago when Christ rose from the dead he completely overcame death and he still lives today (see John 16:20,33). Not only was Jesus brought back to life, he was brought back in a glorified body that would never perish or corrupt (see 1 Corinthians 15:40-49). Everyone else is turning to dust in a grave somewhere.

Second, on many occasions Jesus predicted his own death and resurrection. On a trip through Galilee, Jesus said to his disciples, "The Son of Man is to be delivered into the hands of men, and they will kill Him; and when He has been killed, He will rise three days later" (Mark 9:31). Who else has predicted their own resurrection with such accuracy?

Josh McDowell—Author and speaker

Frequently Asked Questions About the Resurrection

Information

Josh McDowell is a speaker, author and founder of The Josh McDowell Ministry, an organization that reaches young people worldwide with the truth and love of Jesus Christ. He has written or co-written 112 books, which have sold more than 51 million copies worldwide. Josh and his wife, Dottie, have been married 37 years and have four children and two grandchildren.

See Also:

FAQ—*Evidence for the Resurrection*

FAQ—*Jesus Is Alive*

Harmony writes: There are so many different theories about why the tomb was empty that Easter morning, how do we know that the biblical account is true?

Josh says: Those who don't believe the resurrection have found various ways of dealing with the hard fact of the empty tomb. Many people think that the followers of Jesus stole his body and made up the resurrection story. But the news continually shows us that conspiracies eventually unravel. Either the opponents uncover the truth or someone on the inside slips up or gives in to pressure. Yet not one of the disciples, even though they all faced persecution and death, renounced his belief in the resurrection of Jesus.

Harmony: Maybe his followers were just liars. They might not have wanted people to know they took his body.

Josh: Each of the disciples, except John, died a martyr's death. They were persecuted because they tenaciously clung to their beliefs and statements. As Paul Little wrote, "Men will die for what they believe to be true, though it may actually be false. They do not, however, die for what they know is a lie."[2] If the disciples had stolen the body of Jesus, they would have known that their resurrection claim was false. Nevertheless, they never wavered in their commitment to the risen Jesus. Not only did they die for this "lie," but as a testimony to the strength of their convictions, they placed the resurrection of Jesus as the centerpiece of their faith.

If the resurrection was a lie, it seems unrealistic that no disciple would recant it in the face of such harsh suffering. Yet if it was true, as the disciples firmly believed, then they had all the motivation in the world to go to their graves proclaiming the resurrection of Christ. Dr. Moreland notes,

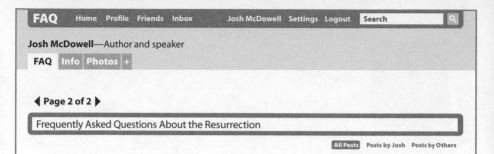
◀ **Page 2 of 2** ▶

Frequently Asked Questions About the Resurrection

All Posts   Posts by Josh   Posts by Others

"They faced hardship, ridicule, hostility, and martyrs' deaths. In light of all this, they could have never sustained such unwavering motivation if they knew what they were preaching was a lie."[3]

Marty writes: Okay, so maybe Jesus' friends didn't take his body. But what about the Jewish or Roman leaders? Didn't they have access to the tomb?

Josh says: Another common theory is that the Roman or Jewish authorities moved the body from the tomb of Joseph of Arimathea to another tomb for safekeeping. Thus, the disciples found the tomb empty and were convinced Jesus had risen. This theory sounds possible until one stops to ask: Why would the authorities do the very thing that caused all of their problems? If the Jewish or Roman authorities had moved the body, then why did they accuse the disciples of stealing it? Such a charge would make no sense. Why would the soldiers have reported the body missing? Why the bribe to cover up what the soldiers saw? If the authorities had custody of the body, they would have happily produced it to stop the resurrection movement.

The most prominent empty-tomb theories have all been carefully examined in light of the elaborate precautions taken at the tomb by the Roman and Jewish authorities. The question remains: What theory best fits all the facts? Only one conclusion takes into account all the facts and does not adjust them to preconceived notions. It is the conclusion that Christ is in fact risen—a supernatural act of God in history.

Sean McDowell—Author and speaker

FAQ Info Photos +

Frequently Asked Questions About the Resurrection

All Posts   Posts by Sean   Posts by Others

Information

Sean McDowell is an author, speaker and the head of the Bible department at Capistrano Valley Christian Schools, where he teaches courses on Apologetics, Theology and Old Testament. He is a popular speaker at camps, churches, schools and conferences nationwide. Sean and his wife, Stephanie, have been married for 8 years and have two children, Scottie and Shauna.

See Also:

FAQ—*Evidence for the Resurrection*

FAQ—*Jesus Is Alive*

Jesse writes: Because the Gospel accounts themselves have contradictions about the actual events, doesn't that disqualify them from being historically accurate?

Sean says: Probably the most common objection to the trustworthiness of the resurrection narratives as found in the Bible is that they contradict and therefore are not reliable historical documents. For example, the four Gospels tell us that Mary was the first to see the risen Jesus, whereas 1 Corinthians 15:5 says that the apostle Peter was the first witness. Mark says the women who went to the tomb to anoint Jesus "saw a young man clothed in a white robe sitting on the right side" (16:4-5), Matthew says an angel was there with a garment "as white as snow" (28:3) and Luke says "two men suddenly appeared to them, clothed in dazzling robes" (24:4).

Jesse: See, these guys couldn't even make up their own minds. Why should I believe what they say?

Sean: It would seem these accounts hopelessly contradict each other, thus destroying their credibility. However, lawyers, philosophers, historians, journalists and others have found that the apparent discrepancies, rather than diminishing the trustworthiness of the Gospels, actually support their reliability.

Journalist William Proctor says that a key principle of journalism is that reporters covering the same story should expect their renditions to be somewhat different, just as we find in the accounts of the four Gospel writers. He explains, "This kind of divergence in stories written about the same events is a common phenomenon when aggressive, independent reporters are at work—for a couple of reasons. First, no one journalist, no matter how skilled, can tell everything that happens in a confusing, fast-moving situation. Each will automatically select facts

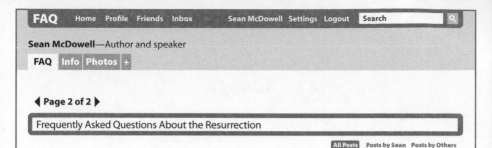

Frequently Asked Questions About the Resurrection

All Posts   Posts by Sean   Posts by Others

based on his or her insights, interests, and biases; consequently, the final stories are bound to be dissimilar. Second, one good reporter may dig a little deeper in one direction than anyone else, and another good reporter may explore in a quite different direction. In this situation, the results will inevitably be somewhat different, even though each report still represents facets of the same story."[4]

Proctor concludes that the biblical account—because of its full agreement on the key facts, in spite of apparent discrepancies—represent the finest kind of journalistic writing. The apparent discrepancies in the Gospel accounts of the resurrection do not invalidate the truth of the event; they actually affirm it. The minor discrepancies of the writers give the unbiased, objective investigator no cause to dismiss the truth of the resurrection accounts as reliable history.

Holly writes: Since most of what we know about the resurrection comes from the Bible, doesn't that disqualify the resurrection as historical fact because we don't know if the documents in the Bible are reliable historically?

Sean says: Because the New Testament makes claims about divine intervention in human affairs, many critics have attacked its reliability. But do they have a basis for their attacks other than their doubt that the miraculous can occur? When scholars look at the number of manuscripts available and how closely they were written to the time of Jesus' death, it becomes abundantly clear that the New Testament is one of the most reliable historical documents known today. F. F. Bruce makes the following observation: "The evidence for our New Testament writings is ever so much greater than the evidence for many writings of classical authors, the authenticity of which no one dreams of questioning. And if the New Testament were a collection of secular writings, their authenticity would generally be regarded as beyond all doubt."[5]

ENDNOTES

Chapter 1: So What?

1. "SuperNinjette," message posted at www.atheistnetwork.com, posted July 16, 2007.

Chapter 2: It's the End of the World as We Know It

1. David Kinnaman, *unChristian: What a New Generation Really Thinks About Christianity* (Grand Rapids, MI: Baker Books, 2007), p. 128.

2. Chap Clark, *Hurt: Inside the World of Today's Teenagers* (Grand Rapids, MI: Baker, 2004), pp. 50, 69.

3. Christian Smith, *Soul Searching* (New York: Oxford University Press, 2005), p. 149. Used by permission of Oxford University Press, www.oup.com.

Chapter 3: Love Is a Verb

1. Philip Yancey, *Disappointment with God* (Grand Rapids, MI: Zondervan, 1988), p. 122.

Chapter 4: Our Greatest Hopes and Fears

1. These points were developed in Stephen T. Davis, *Risen Indeed* (Grand Rapids, MI: Eerdmans, 1993), pp. 203-204. Reprinted by permission of the publisher. All rights reserved.

2. N. T. Wright, as quoted in Randy Alcorn, *Heaven* (Carol Stream, IL: Tyndale, 2004), p. 409.

3. Alcorn, *Heaven*, pp. 10-12

4. Ibid., p. 241.

5. Dan Kimball, *They Like Jesus but Not the Church* (Grand Rapids, MI: Zondervan, 2007), p. 69.

6. David Kinnaman, *unChristian: What a New Generation Really Thinks about Christianity* (Grand Rapids, MI: Baker Books, 2007), pp. 27, 185.

7. Jean M. Twenge, *Generation Me* (New York: Free Press, 2006), p. 110.

8. "U.S. Divorce Statistics," *Divorce Magazine,* http://www.divorcemagazine.com/statistics/statsUS.shtml (accessed October 2008).

Chapter 5: The Event That Changed History

1. N. T. Wright, *Jesus and the Victory of God* (Minneapolis, MN: Augsburg Fortress Press, 1997), pp. 551-552.

2. James Montgomery Boice, *The Gospel of John: Triumph Through Tragedy* (Grand Rapids, MI: Baker Book House, 1999), p. 1472.

3. Haim Cohn, "Reflections on the Trial of Jesus," in *Judaism*, vol. 20, 1971, p. 11.

4. Craig A. Evans, "What Did Jesus Do?" in *Jesus Under Fire* (Grand Rapids, MI: Zondervan, 1995), p. 29.

5. In *The Antiquities*, Josephus refers to Jesus' trial and crucifixion under Pontius Pilate. Although the passage in which this information appears is hotly debated, most scholars agree that Josephus wrote a basic text (which includes the reference to Pilate) to which later Christians made additions.

6. Dr. Alexander Metherell was interviewed by Lee Strobel in *The Case for Christ* (Grand Rapids, MI: Zondervan, 1998), pp. 197-198.

7. English translation by Michael W. Holmes in Michael W. Holmes, *The Apostolic Fathers: Greek Texts and English Translations*, second edition (Grand Rapids, MI: Baker, 1999), p. 227.

8. J. W. Hewitt, "The Use of Nails in the Crucifixion," *Harvard Theological Review*, vol. 25, 1932, pp. 29-45.

9. N. Haas, "Anthropological Observations on the Skeletal Remains from Giv' at ha-Mivtar," *Israel Exploration Journal* vol. 20, 1970, p. 57.

10. Cicero, *Orations*, Speech 13, 12:27; *Gospel of Peter* 4:14.

11. See William D. Edwards, Wesley J. Gabel and Floyd E. Hosmer, "On the Physical Death of Jesus Christ," pp. 1462-1463; C. Truman Davis, "The Crucifixion of Jesus," *Arizona Medicine*, March 1965, pp. 185-186; Stuart Bergsma, "Did Jesus Die of a Broken Heart?" *The Calvin Forum*, March 1948, p. 165; Alexander Metherell in Lee Strobel, *The Case for Christ*, p. 199.

12. Michael Green, *Man Alive* (Downers Grove, IL: InterVarsity Press, 1968), p. 33.

13. Ibid., p. 573.

14. John Dominic Crossan, *Who Killed Jesus?* (New York: Harper Collins, 1996), p. 5.

Chapter 6: Fact vs. Fiction

1. Henry Sumner Maine, *Ancient Law* (New York: Henry Holt and Company, 1888), p. 203.

2. Paul L. Maier, "The Empty Tomb as History," *Christianity Today*, vol. 19, March 28, 1975, p. 5.

3. Michael Grant, *Jesus: An Historian's Review of the Gospels* (New York: Charles Scribner's Sons, 1977), p. 176.

4. Bill White, *A Thing Incredible* (Israel: Yanetz Ltd., 1976).

5. Reginald H. Fuller, *The Foundations of New Testament Christology* (New York: Scribner's, 1965), p. 142.

6. Gary R. Habermas, *The Historical Jesus: Ancient Evidence for the Life of Christ* (Joplin, MO: College Press, 1996), chapter 7.

7. Norman L. Geisler, *Baker Encyclopedia of Christian Apologetics* (Grand Rapids, MI: Baker Books, 1999), p. 654.

8. Craig, *The Son Rises*, pp. 94-95.

9. Merril C. Tenney, "The Resurrection of Jesus Christ," in *Prophecy in the Making*, edited by Carl Henry (Carol Stream, IL: Creation House, 1971), p. 59.

10. Josephus, *Antiquities* 20:200; see Gary Habermas and Michael Licona, *The Case for the Resurrection* (Grand Rapids, MI: Kregel Publishers, 2004), p. 68.

11. This comment was made in a conversation with Josh McDowell, January 1981.

12. See Josh McDowell, *The New Evidence That Demands a Verdict* (Nashville, TN: Thomas Nelson, 1999) for detailed information on these various manuscript discoveries.

13. Craig Blomberg, "Where Do We Start Studying Jesus?" *Jesus Under Fire* (Grand Rapids, MI: Zondervan, 1995), p. 29.

14. Ibid., pp. 29-30.

15. Frederick G. Kenyon, *The Bible and Archaeology* (New York: Harper and Row, 1940), p. 288.

16. John A. T. Robinson, *Can We Trust the New Testament?* (Grand Rapids, MI: Eerdmans, 1977), p. 36. Reprinted by permission of the publisher. All rights reserved.

17. John Ankerburg and John Weldon, *Knowing the Truth About the Resurrection* (Eugene, OR: Harvest House, 1996), p. 20.

18. William F. Albright, *The Archaeology of Palestine*, revised edition (Baltimore, MD: Penguin Books, 1960), p. 141.

19. F. F. Bruce, "Archaeological Confirmation of the New Testament," in *Revelation and the Bible*, edited by Carl Henry (Grand Rapids, MI: Baker Book House, 1969), p. 329.

20. Markus Bockmuehl, *This Jesus: Martyr, Lord, Messiah* (Downers Grove, IL: InterVarsity Press, 1996), pp. 70-71.

21. Gary R. Habermas, *The Historical Jesus: Ancient Evidence for the Life of Christ* (Joplin, MO: College Press, 1996), p. 224.
22. Gary R. Habermas, "Why I Believe the New Testament Is Historically Reliable," in *Why I Am a Christian: Leading Thinkers Explain Why They Believe*, edited by Norman L. Geisler and Paul K. Hoffman (Grand Rapids, MI: Baker Books, 2001), p. 150.
23. Edwin Yamauchi, "Jesus Outside the New Testament: What Is the Evidence?" in *Jesus Under Fire*, pp. 221-222.
24. Gary R. Habermas, "Why I Believe the New Testament Is Historically Reliable," in Geisler and Hoffman, *Why I Am a Christian*, pp. 157-158.
25. Josh McDowell, *The New Evidence That Demands a Verdict* (Nashville, TN: Thomas Nelson, 1999).

Frequently Asked Questions About the Resurrection
1. Richard Purtill, "Defining Miracles," taken from *In Defense of Miracles*, edited by R. Douglas Geivett and Gary R. Habermas. © 1977 by R. Douglas Geivett and Gary R. Habermas. Published by InterVarsity Press, P.O. Box 1400, Downers Grove, IL 60515, pp. 62-63.
2. Paul Little, *Know Why You Believe* (Wheaton, IL: Scripture Press, 1967), p. 173.
3. J. P. Moreland, *Scaling the Secular City: A Defense of Christianity* (Grand Rapids, MI: Baker Academic, 1987), p. 172.
4. William Proctor, *The Resurrection Report* (Nashville, TN: B&H Publishers, 2000), p. 41.
5. F. F. Bruce, *The New Testament Documents: Are They Reliable?* fifth edition (Downer's Grove, IL: InterVarsity Press, 1960), p. 15.

ALSO AVAILABLE FROM JOSH McDOWELL AND SEAN McDOWELL

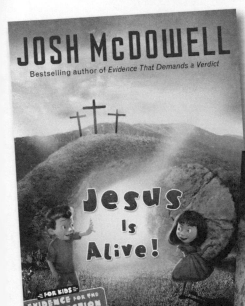

Jesus Is Alive!
Evidence for the Resurrection for Kids
Josh McDowell and *Sean McDowell*
with *Gwen Ellis*
ISBN 978.08307.47863
ISBN 08307.47869

Evidence for the Resurrection
Josh McDowell and *Sean McDowell*
ISBN 978.08307.47856
ISBN 08307.47850

Available at Bookstores Everywhere!